Left Behind After The Rapture

by Susan Davis

© Copyright 2013 – Susan Davis

ISBN-13: 978-1482605815

ISBN-10: 1482605813

NOTICE: You are encouraged to distribute copies of this document through any means, electronic or in printed form. You may post this material, in whole or in part, on your website or anywhere else. But we do request that you include this notice so others may know they can copy and distribute as well. This book is available as a free ebook and mp3 at the website:

http://end-times-prophecy.com

© 2013 by Susan Davis

All Scripture reference and notes are from the King James Version Bible.

TABLE OF CONTENTS

1. So Many Are Asleep — 5
2. I Will Not Settle For Second Place — 9
3. There Is No Changing The Course Of History Now — 18
4. Calamity Will Reach An Unheard Of Plateau — 54
5. Cannot Wait On MY Bride Forever — 79
6. Outside Of My Will, All Men Practice Evil — 97
7. People Believe My Warnings And My Words Are A Joke — 100
8. Anything Can Become An Idol — 105
9. I Am True To My Words — 111
10. There Is No Other By Which You Can Be Saved — 117
11. The Churches Are The Devil's Playground — 130
12. Evil Is Even Invading The Places That Should Be Safe — 137

ABOUT THESE PROPHECIES

Susan operates in the gift of prophecy. In 1 Corinthians 14:1 it states, "Follow the way of love and eagerly desire gifts of the Spirit, especially prophecy." Now we are living and supposed to be obeying God's instructions in the New Testament. Although some believe that spiritual gifts, such as prophecies, have been done away with, this is man's thinking and not God's. God has not changed His covenant. We are still living in the era of the New Covenant – which is also called the New Testament. Please understand that your first commitment should be to the Lord Jesus Christ and His Word as written in the Bible – especially the New Testament.

As always, all prophecy needs to be tested against the Bible. However, if the prophecy lines up with the Bible then we are expected to obey it. Currently God does not use prophecies to introduce new doctrines. They are used to reinforce what God has already given to us in the Bible. God also uses them to give us individual warnings of future events that will affect us.

Just like in the Old Testament, God uses prophets in the New Testament times of which we are currently in. The book of Acts, which is in the New Testament, mentions some of the prophets such as Judas and Silas (Acts 15:32) and Agabus (Acts 21:21) and there were others. The ministry of prophets is also mentioned in New Testament times in 1 Corinthians 12:28, 14:1,29,32,37 as well as in Ephesians 2:20,3:5,4:11.

Jesus chooses prophets to work for Him on earth. Among other things, Jesus uses prophecies and prophets to communicate His desires to His children. The Bible itself was written prophetically through the inspiration of the Holy Spirit.

Some people say words of prophecy are in danger of adding to the Bible or taking from it -- well the Bible speaks of prophecy as being a Gift of the HOLY SPIRIT. The way the Bible is added to or taken from is not through additional words of prophecy received by the people which the HOLY SPIRIT gives words to, but by the changing of GOD's concepts to add new unBiblical concepts from other pagan beliefs for example. But the primary work of the prophets in the Bible has always been to focus the people back to GOD's WORD, the BIBLE.

As it says in 1 Thessalonians 5:19-21, "Do not put out the Spirit's fire; do not treat prophecies with contempt. Test everything. Hold on to the good." And the way to test the messages is to compare it's content to what the Bible says.

In all the prophecies below I personally (Mike Peralta - Book Preparer) have tested these messages and they are all in agreement to what the Bible says. But you must also test these messages, yourself, to the Bible. And if they are consistent with the Bible, then God expects that you will take them to heart and obey His instructions.

1. So Many Are Asleep

Sun, 7 Oct 2012

Words of the LORD: "I Cannot Open Eyes Fast Enough: So Many Are Asleep."

The LORD's Words for Today (Posted at www.End-Times-Prophecy.Com)

Dear Faithful Followers of CHRIST:

Children, your LORD has Words for you:

There is a lot of turmoil about the day ahead. Some believe MY Coming is near. Not enough believe this. There are not enough who believe this. Many believe this world will sustain them into the future. They are not keeping their eyes fixed on ME. I am the ONLY ANSWER to a troubled world—a deeply troubled world.

You need to prepare your hearts as the days are growing dark. It is no mistake that the human race is turning a corner—heading into deep, dark depravity. I am not going to take out with ME rebellious children when I come for MY beautiful bride and I AM COMING!

These are the ones who will be the most, saddest: MY lukewarm church and those who lead them astray. Do not despair MY holy church—those who pursue me above all else: worldly pursuits; idols of the world; all the things that cause your heart to go astray.

The warnings are winding down, because MY Coming is close. Stop relying on your earthly gods to lead you. I am the ONE, TRUE, LOYAL GOD. Only those who are watching will come with ME. Church prepare: your salvation is at hand.

The CRUCIFIED ONE,

YESHUA HA MASHIACH.

(Words received from the LORD by Susan, October 5, 2012)

Words of the LORD:

"I am not going to bring back to life a world full of hatred for ME."

(Words Received from Our LORD by Susan, October 1, 2012)

It is time again for a letter:

Children your hour draws near for MY Return. I am coming with haste.

The world is growing darker. Few want to believe this is happening. Many want to embrace the world. Few want to believe I am going to do what I say I will do. Few want to believe that I am a GOD of truth. I have laid out MY Plans and they are coming to pass.

The world is withering like the fig tree. It withers. The oppression of sin is bringing it down. I am allowing the fig tree to wither. It is time for that which cannot produce fruit to die, to allow the death of a dying, decaying, and sinful world.

I am not going to revive the unrevivable. I am not going to bring back to life a world full of hatred for ME. I am going to allow this world to come to the end of itself. I am going to remove the few who still have life in them, the few who still trust in ME—who live in ME fully. The rest will face the demise of dying fig tree: what the world looks like when I, GOD pull away MY Life-giving Hand.

Those left behind will surely see what life on a dying planet looks like. I am going to walk away from the earth and allow it to fall under the decay of sin and corruption and the rule of rebellion will reign. This is a world that knows not GOD. This is the world coming for MY left behind church and sinful men who reject their GOD.

This is the hour of darkness that is coming: bleak and foreboding. You only have a few hours of daylight left to make your way to MY Guiding Hand. Run into MY Arms quickly before the door closes and your lamps go out and darkness moves in.

Make peace with your GOD. Lay your life at MY Feet. Surrender your heart and soul. I have little time to give you now before MY enemy moves in to swallow up the daylight. The lion is roaring: moving about to see who he can devour. Protect yourself with MY Blood. MY Precious Blood is your only hope.

Follow ME out to safety. You have minutes before all goes black. Don't fight MY Love—give in to it. I am the only STRONG TOWER—FORTRESS over mankind—SAVING FORCE.

Pull free from sin—run to salvation.

This is the SAVIOR to mankind,

EVERLASTING...FAITHFUL...MESSIAH...SAVIOR.

Matthew 21:18-19: [18]Now in the morning as HE returned into the city, HE hungered. [19]And when HE saw a fig tree in the way, HE came to it, and found nothing thereon, but leaves only, and said unto it, Let no fruit grow on thee henceforward forever. And presently the fig tree withered away.

Mark 11:11-13: [11]And JESUS entered into Jerusalem, and into the temple: and when HE had looked round about upon all things, and now the eventide was come, HE went out unto Bethany with the twelve. [12]And on the morrow, when they were come from Bethany, HE was hungry: [13]And seeing a fig tree afar off having leaves, HE came, if haply HE might find anything thereon: and when HE came to it, HE found nothing but leaves; for the time of figs was not yet.

Mark 11:19-21: [19]And when even was come, HE went out of the city. [20]And in the morning, as they passed by, they saw the fig tree dried up from the roots.[21]And Peter calling to remembrance saith unto HIM, MASTER, behold, the fig tree which thou cursedst is withered away.

2. I Will Not Settle For Second Place

Words Received from Our LORD by Susan, October 2, 2012

Let US Begin:

Listen closely as I give you Words.

MY children—as you know the world is changing rapidly. There is a flood of darkness moving over the land. I cannot open eyes fast enough—so many are asleep. Soon the evil one will have his way with this world and the people will be caught off guard—completely asleep. They will be taken and apprehended with little trouble by the evil that is taking over.

Only a few now are really watching and seeing the trouble moving over the land. There is only a few who pursue ME so that their lamps are filled and their eyes are opened by the Light, the Light of MY Truth and MY HOLY SPIRIT. HE is the ONE WHO Enlightens. HE is the ONE WHO Fills the oil lamps and brings the Truth into the open. Only MY SPIRIT enables the people to come to ME in fullness holding nothing back from ME, GOD.

Without a complete filling of MY SPIRIT, and a partially filled lamp, you will not see the horrors coming and you will not see the remedy to avoiding the trouble coming your way. It is by MY Lamp Oil—MY Fullness of SPIRIT that you are made ready.

To have a full lamp and a SPIRIT-Filled life you must empty yourself to make room for MY SPIRIT. You must empty your soul of the pleasures and desires for this world. The pursuits of this world will consume your heart, take over your mind, and fill you so that there is no time left for ME, your GOD.

Remember: I am a Jealous GOD—I will not settle for second place in your life! In its place, I bring wholeness, I bring stability, I bring love and contentment. Your feet are placed on the SOLID ROCK. There is no shadow of turning in MY Ways. You do not need to doubt, by faith—your foundation in GOD.

I build your life on a firm foundation: stability of mind. Your heart will not fluctuate or be double-minded. Stay in MY Presence and I will bring you the peace of GOD. You never need to worry again, because MY Love and Security towers over you—protects you from evil and I show you the safe and narrow passage to eternal life and salvation.

Run into MY Waiting Arms—this world is growing dark and controlled by the spirit of the antichrist. I will bring MY bride out to safety. If you focus on ME, I will keep you under MY Wings of protection. I can be relied upon. I can be trusted. There is no reason to fear—only those who know ME not have much to fear and little to look forward to: without ME—MY Blood Covering and Presence of Strength all men would be lost.

I am looking for people who so love their GOD they are willing to walk free of their traditions of men and the commitments life places that distracts from time spent with ME, GOD. You, however, must choose how you spend your time—the free time you are given. Is it to get to know ME better or do you allow other things to come between US?

I cannot take those who do not know ME out to MY Heavenly Home. Think this over carefully. You decide: will you come with ME when I call out MY church or stay for the worst time known to men? This is the hour of discernment. Pray for MY Eyesalve. Pray for MY Truth and a clean heart so that you will be found worthy to stand before ME by MY Pure Blood Covering.

I plead for you before MY FATHER. Let ME save you now before it is too late.

I am the SAVIOR of mankind.

KING of kings, LORD of lords.

"I AM"

1 Thessalonians 5:6: ⁶Therefore let us not sleep, as do others; but let us watch and be sober.

Matthew 25:3-4: ³They that were foolish took their lamps, and took no oil with them: ⁴But the wise took oil in their vessels with their lamps.

Deuteronomy 4:24: ²⁴For the LORD thy GOD is a CONSUMING FIRE, even a JEALOUS GOD.

1 John 4:3: ³And every spirit that confesseth not that JESUS CHRIST is come in the flesh is not of GOD: and this is that spirit of antichrist, whereof ye have heard that it should come; and even now already is it in the world.

Revelation 3:18: ¹⁸I counsel thee to buy of me gold tried in the fire, that thou mayest be rich; and white raiment, that thou mayest be clothed, and that the shame of thy nakedness do not appear; and anoint thine eyes with eyesalve, that thou mayest see.

James 4:8: ⁸Draw nigh to GOD, and HE will draw nigh to you. Cleanse your hands, ye sinners; and purify your hearts, ye double minded.

Rote Worship Of The Lukewarm Church

Wed, 17 Oct 2012

The LORD's Words: "There is no changing the course of history now."

The LORD's Words for Today (Posted at www.End-Times-Prophecy.Com)

Dear Faithful Followers of CHRIST:

The LORD recently gave me this Word: "Love that is not passionate: is not loving." He continued to talk about the rote worship of the lukewarm church and how the people in the church pews during worship go through their rote routines and think about what they are preparing to eat that day or the football game they will watch later but not about the LORD. I can't help but to think of the passion of our LORD on the day HE gave HIS ALL on Calvary through all sorts of horror and torment. Really what could be more passionate than for GOD above to do this for mankind? I think then of the verse in Revelation of the stark reality of what CHRIST will do ultimately with the lukewarm church:

Revelation 3:16: So then because thou art lukewarm, and neither cold nor hot, I will spue thee out of MY Mouth.

With all the events of the world pointing to a near rapture, the Words I received recently from the LORD should be most troubling to you if you are not focused on HIM. The LORD said to me that those who will be raptured will be like a morsel next to a banquet (trust me, I don't think like this...).

What is the cause for so many to be in a lukewarm state and not ready for the LORD's Return? I believe it is clearly because the world has a much bigger hold on people than the LORD who created them. Here are some verses from the bible that plainly state that you cannot serve two masters—both GOD and the world—and there is no third acceptable state of being:

Matthew 6:24: No man can serve two masters: for either he will hate the one, and love the other; or else he will hold to the one, and despise the other. Ye cannot serve GOD and mammon.

John 17:14: I have given them THY Word; and the world hath hated them, because they are not of the world, even as I am not of the world.

Romans 12:2: And be not conformed to this world: but be ye transformed by the renewing of your mind, that ye may prove what is that good, and acceptable, and perfect, will of GOD.

1 Corinthians 2:12: Now we have received, not the spirit of the world, but the SPIRIT which is of GOD; that we might know the things that are freely given to us of GOD.

2 Corinthians 4:4: In whom the god of this world hath blinded the minds of them which believe not, lest the light of the glorious gospel of CHRIST, WHO is the image of GOD, should shine unto them.

The bible has many verses that talk about the narrow path (that few find) to the LORD such as this one:

Matthew 7:14: Because strait is the gate, and narrow is the way, which leadeth unto life, and few there be that find it.

It is the world and the worship of worldly idols that keep people from putting CHRIST FIRST in their lives. Here are some unsuspected idols that keep people from putting GOD first in their lives:

Unsuspected idols: idol worship of country—idol worship of children—idol worship of your own future plans—idol worship of church/religion—idol worship of a false image of god (believing in some of the scriptures but picking and choosing what to believe)—idol worship of worries/cares/troubles—idol worship: anything that takes your primary focus off of god including worldly pursuits: entertainment, family, career.

Very Few Are Interested In My Love And My Warnings

Words of the LORD:

"MY rebellious children are filled with spirits of the antichrist that will lead them to their ultimate destruction."

(Words Received from Our LORD by Susan, October 8, 2012)

Let US Begin:

Today children, I want to give you new Words.

The world is coming apart for sure. If you haven't noticed then you are not looking. There is a tragedy playing out, a great tragic play. I wrote this play a long time ago—in the Words of MY Book, MY Word. Now you are seeing this story unfold. It is undeniably happening. You are part of that story…

You are a key player in these...the last days. Many are written about: those who reject ME...those who turn from ME...those who run to MY enemy and the world for their relief and answers. They are turning in their hearts to evil governing and leadership because they believe this is where their answers lie. All this will lead to destruction, if you embrace evil for your answers. Then you will have a sad ending. If you look to MY Light for your answers, then you will find relief, safety, and safe-keeping.

I also have those in MY Book who represent MY bride: MY true church. She has forsaken all others for ME, her GROOM. She has cast down all other gods in her heart and only seeks ME, the MASTER of her soul. I am the undisputed LEADER of her heart. All others are controlled by other spirits of MY enemy: spirits of pride; addiction; lust for the world; blaspheming GOD; fear; revenge; bitterness; un-forgiveness, adultery; witchcraft; rebellion; murder.

MY rebellious children are filled with spirits of the antichrist that will lead them to their ultimate destruction. They only want to hear lying spirits and not the True Word that comes from the Mouth of MY HOLY SPIRIT WHO resides within MY bride and true church.

There is a battle going on much darker than anything you can see with the visible eye—this battle rages all around you. It is the battle for your very soul—the enemy has launched a well-laid attack against you. He has put out every trap for you MY children to fall into. Only with a full oil lamp can you see the hidden mines that MY enemy has set out for you—only with a full lamp will you see the destruction that lies ahead.

If your light is weak and your lamp oil is not full you cannot see the traps set out for you to fall into. Without the full power of MY SPIRIT operating in your spirit by making a full and complete surrender to

ME, you cannot survive what is coming right at the door. The full oil lamp that is given in exchange for a full surrender is the Light, the Truth that lights the way down the narrow path that leads to MY Coming Rescue. Only this full surrender—a death to self—empties your spirit to make room for MY SPIRIT to come within you to fill your lamp and give you eyes to see the great traps and mines laid by MY enemy for your demise. He comes to kill, steal, and destroy you. He is bent on destruction of all MY children. Many have fallen into his hands. Many more will very soon.

I am warning you because I love you. Very few are interested in MY Love and MY Warnings. They are greatly deceived by MY enemy and by the noise and distraction of the world. You must come away from the world and all its noise and get quiet with your GOD. Get to know ME in a quiet secret place, where I can reveal MY Heart to you and lead you to Truth through the pages of MY Book.

The hour is closing down. Come to terms with MY Pleadings. Accept this lifeline I am throwing you—it is MY nail-pierced Hand and MY Blood-Soaked Cross. This is MY Salvation. This is what I, GOD did for mankind. Only MY Love is complete and sufficient for all the unmet needs of mankind.

Come in humble submission—earnest repentance. Seek MY Face. I will forgive and refresh you and you will join ME in MY Kingdom—Everlasting Beauty.

I am ready to take hold of you and bring you out—are you coming?

This is GOD COMPASSIONATE,

THE LAMB AND THE LION.

2 Timothy 3:16-17: All scripture is given by inspiration of GOD, and is profitable for doctrine, for reproof, for correction, for instruction in righteousness:

Proverbs 1:24-33: [24]Because I have called, and ye refused; I have stretched out MY Hand, and no man regarded; [25]But ye have set at nought all MY Counsel, and would none of MY Reproof: [26]I also will laugh at your calamity; I will mock when your fear cometh; [27]When your fear cometh as desolation, and your destruction cometh as a whirlwind; when distress and anguish cometh upon you. [28]Then shall they call upon ME, but I will not answer; they shall seek ME early, but they shall not find ME: [29]For that they hated knowledge, and did not choose the fear of the LORD: [30]They would none of MY Counsel: they despised all MY Reproof. [31]Therefore shall they eat of the fruit of their own way, and be filled with their own devices. [32]For the turning away of the simple shall slay them, and the prosperity of fools shall destroy them. [33]But whoso hearkeneth unto ME shall dwell safely, and shall be quiet from fear of evil.

1 Samuel 15:23: For rebellion is as the sin of witchcraft, and stubbornness is as iniquity and idolatry. Because thou hast rejected the Word of the LORD, HE hath also rejected thee from being king.

John 10:10: The thief cometh not, but for to steal, and to kill, and to destroy: I am come that they might have life, and that they might have it more abundantly.

Psalm 91:1: He that dwelleth in the secret place of the MOST HIGH shall abide under the shadow of the ALMIGHTY.

3. There Is No Changing The Course Of History Now

Words of the LORD:

"There is no changing the course of history now."

(Words Received from Our LORD by Susan, October 10, 2012)

Let US Begin:

Children, I am GOD Everlasting—I Rule over the nations.

I am Coming to take MY Own with ME. I have prepared a place for MY bride. It is a wonderful place in MY Heavenlies.

Soon those who are ready are coming. They are coming out to live in the mansions I have made for them. There are going to be wonderful things to look forward to—beauty that is indescribable.

MY children, listen carefully as I proceed to tell you how to be ready for MY Coming:

I want you to make a FULL surrender to ME.

I want you to repent to ME sincerely from the heart.

I want you to forgive all those around leaving nothing undone.

I want you to have complete filling of MY HOLY SPIRIT releasing worldly pursuits in exchange for a full fledge relationship with your GOD. Come to know ME—spend time with ME. Give ME your all in all—holding nothing back.

Too many will be left behind to face a grossly deteriorating world falling into the hands of MY enemy. You cannot love ME and mammon both—you will love one and hate the other. You don't get it both ways as MY lukewarm church believes.

There is no changing the course of history now. The world is starting to fall apart with evil leaders all around. You must decide: are you coming out when I call you up? Will you choose for ME or MY enemy and the world he rules?

What can I do to persuade you that destruction is coming to the land and this is because the world has chosen to embrace evil instead of their GOD?

Why do people believe that this world holds answers for them when there is so much sadness at every turn? What is so convincing about the evil and sorrow everywhere that would cause you to believe that MY Love, GOD's Love, isn't sufficient for you?

I have a plan for your life. It is to give you a hope and a future, but I can't take you into MY Heavenlies if you decide against ME—the surrender must be complete and full or WE will part company and you may be lost in sudden destruction.

Choose for ME and let ME save your soul. I am the GOD WHO delivers. I delivered during Noah's time…Lot's time…and Moses' time…and I will deliver again.

I AM the GREAT.

"I AM"

Psalm 66:7: HE ruleth by HIS power forever; HIS Eyes behold the nations: let not the rebellious exalt themselves. Selah.

Ephesians 6:12: For we wrestle not against flesh and blood, but against principalities, against powers, against the rulers of the darkness of this world, against spiritual wickedness in high places.

Luke 17:26-30: ^{26}And as it was in the days of Noah, so shall it be also in the days of the SON of man. ^{27}They did eat, they drank, they married wives, they were given in marriage, until the day that Noah entered into the ark, and the flood came, and destroyed them all. ^{28}Likewise also as it was in the days of Lot; they did eat, they drank, they bought, they sold, they planted, they builded; ^{29}But the same day that Lot went out of Sodom it rained fire and brimstone from heaven, and destroyed them all. ^{30}Even thus shall it be in the day when the SON of man is revealed.

1 Thessalonians 5:3: For when they shall say, Peace and safety; then sudden destruction cometh upon them, as travail upon a woman with child; and they shall not escape.

Isaiah 13:11: And I will punish the world for their evil, and the wicked for their iniquity; and I will cause the arrogancy of the proud to cease, and will lay low the haughtiness of the terrible.

Matthew 13:22: He also that received seed among the thorns is he that heareth the word; and the care of this world, and the deceitfulness of riches, choke the word, and he becometh unfruitful.

This Important Letter from the LORD was received by a subscriber, Hafsa Rashid: Shalom, I hope this will bless you and draw you even closer to the LORD JESUS:

"The time has now come for MY soon descending on this earth to take my ransomed bride. Who is my bride: the one who has kept her gown pure, clean, wrinkle-free, without spot. The one who has preserved and not desired the pleasures of this world: that is my bride.

Many are asleep, planning for their future without ME. How do you plan for a future without ME, how possible is this, yet my word is so clear on what you first love should be or have you forgotten I am the Truth, the Way, and the Life.

Has my enemy blinded you to an extent that you cannot see the evil that surrounds you? Does MY Word not say the devil looks for who, he might devour (John 10:10: the thief only comes only to steal and kill and destroy; I have come that they may have life and have it to the full.)

Cry out and seek ME and I will release MY SPIRIT and this veil of blindness will come out so that you can see how this world has turned against ME. I can no longer continue to see MY own turn against me, yet I paid a great price. I died a horrible death in the very hands of MY children. Yet you still assume this was nothing.

Awake you, who slumber, for the time is neigh, be watchful lest you fall into the hands of MY enemy. The door is still open for those who are willing to come to ME. I stand at the door knocking: those who hear and open, I will come in and dwell in them. Those who reject MY Call, them will I also abandon when I come to retrieve MY bride.

Awake O' slumbering bride. How can a bride who is preparing for her wedding be asleep? Isn't she to be preparing and keeping herself ready for the most beautiful and glorious day of her life, to be united together with her BRIDEGROOM. The price has been paid, the gown is still dirty, cleanse yourself up MY bride, for I can only solemnize with a clean, wrinkle-, and spot-free bride. This is the one I come for.

Awake and be watchful for the day draws near for MY Coming!"

This message was received at 1:00 A.M., 10th October 2012.

Shalom, Hafsa Rashid

Letter and Vision from a Reader: Sister Susan, Today 10th October, I saw a golden crown that appeared from heaven and was spinning until it disappeared and I was the only one that saw it. Please what does it signify? I care to know. Please reply. GOD bless you.

Word from the LORD regarding this vision: This is truly a sign of MY Coming--I am coming for a royal bride who is looking up for ME. All others will be left. You can count on this vision it is reliable.

MY Will - Only Here Is Where You Are Safe

Thu, 25 Oct 2012

The LORD's Words: "You are for MY enemy if you are against ME and not in MY Will."

The LORD's Words for Today (Posted at www.End-Times-Prophecy.Com)

Dear Faithful Followers of CHRIST:

Matthew 22:1-5: And JESUS answered and spake unto them again by parables, and said,[2] The Kingdom of Heaven is like unto a certain king, which made a marriage for his son,[3] And sent forth his servants to call them that were bidden to the wedding: and they would not come.[4] Again, he sent forth other servants, saying, Tell them which are bidden, Behold, I have prepared my dinner: my oxen and my fatlings are killed, and all things are ready: come unto the marriage.5 But they made light of it, and went their ways, one to his farm, another to his merchandise:

Recently, I was just reading over the headlines on the latest edition of the End Times News Report we put out and I was amazed. And I thought to myself: "How could anyone actually look at these headlines and not get that we are in the end times and the LORD's Return is imminent?" World war is on the horizon and Israel is right in the center of the action—but don't forget that when the LORD Returns the people will be in their quiet routines, according to scripture. And yet, Christians and church pastors still want to talk about being here many years into the future...but this too is Bible prophecy that the people will be caught off guard—the vast majority of them...

Words of the LORD:

"Open your eyes and look at the changing world moving to all antichrist ways and beliefs."

(Words Received from Our LORD by Susan, October 18, 2012)

Daughter, it is I, your LORD from up above:

The hour is drawing near and I am getting even closer. There is no doubt that MY Coming is close. I do not want MY children to be in despair when they have so much to look forward to after I remove them to their new homes and safekeeping in MY skies.

There is safety under MY Skirts. This is where you are safe. Do not believe you can find safety anywhere else. Come to the center of MY Will—only here is where you are safe. There is no other place to safety. All other places lead to destruction and eternal loss. Why do you cling so to the idea that the world holds answers to your longing heart—a heart always longing for answers to the troubles of this world?

Don't succumb to the ways of this world. For a time it all looks so right, but if you allow yourself to be led away to the lies and deceit of a world outside of MY Will—your destruction is sure and founded. Your demise is set and your ending is sure.

Only MY Will, MY Way, MY Truth leading down the narrow path will lead you to life everlasting in MY Kingdom of Holiness and Peace. There is a world out there pulling you away from ME. It is designed by MY enemy to distract and deceive you. Come away from it all. Find your way to MY narrow path.

I will not delay MY Coming much longer. The world is growing so dark. Soon you will not be able to see your hands before your face—the evil and darkness will be so thick. Darkness is all around you. Open your eyes and look at the changing world moving to all antichrist ways and beliefs. MY Beautiful Word and Truth will soon be snuffed out by the antichrist spirit moving through the world.

MY bride will be removed and those left will face the greatest corruption and terror mankind has ever known. You can avoid this nightmare. Cling to your LORD…run under MY Skirts. Press into ME for all Truth, to have your eyes opened and ears opened to Truth. Now is the time to get to know your GOD—not later…later will be too late.

Turn to ME in full surrender. Repent to ME of all sin. Show ME love and forgiveness for others around you. Come to ME for a filling of MY SPIRIT. HE will lead you to peace and safety, wholeness and healing.

The world is decaying, crumbling. Soon it will be a dying ember. Come out to safekeeping with ME—HUMBLE SAVIOR...MY Name is HOSANNA—HIGHER POWER

John 12:25: He that loveth his life shall lose it; and he that hateth his life in this world shall keep it unto life eternal.

Matthew 23:37: O Jerusalem, Jerusalem, thou that killest the prophets, and stonest them which are sent unto thee, how often would I have gathered thy children together, even as a hen gathereth her chickens under her wings, and ye would not!

Matthew 7:14: Because strait is the gate, and narrow is the way, which leadeth unto life, and few there be that find it.

1 John 4:3: And every spirit that confesseth not that JESUS CHRIST is come in the flesh is not of GOD: and this is that spirit of antichrist, whereof ye have heard that it should come; and even now already is it in the world.

Words of the LORD:

"You are for MY enemy if you are against ME and not in MY Will."

(Words Received from Our LORD by Susan, October 19, 2012)

Listen to MY Words—write down these Words:

The world is about to fall into chaos. It is the chaos of MY enemy. It is the chaos of evil. Peace...love...protection all come from GOD. Evil breeds anarchy, chaos, and rebellion. This is the difference between MY Kingdom of GOD and MY enemy's kingdom of evil.

If you choose against ME, you are for MY enemy no matter what else you believe. You are for MY enemy if you are against ME and not in MY Will. Even those who attend church, appear religious, are devils if they are lukewarm and lost in their ways. Does not MY Word say it?

You can make for yourself a million excuses to run apart from MY Perfect Will and appease yourself believing all is well between us, but many are now in hell who have also believed this. A dance with the devil can take on many different looks. That is why he is so deceptive and cunning. Apart from MY Will you work for MY enemy no matter how righteous you believe yourself. A little bit of leaven spoils the whole lump.

You cannot conquer this sin in this world in the flesh apart from a complete filling of MY HOLY SPIRIT though many try and believe differently. Many will die in their own efforts and enter hell. So many come into MY Presence believing all is well between us only to discover that outside of MY Perfect Will for their life lies death and destruction and eternal hell.

How do you know if you are in MY Perfect Will?

There is only ONE WAY: come to ME and make a full surrender—give ME ALL including your future plans and your personal will. Let ME cover you in MY Precious Blood and fill you completely with MY HOLY SPIRIT. Ask for a complete filling of MY SPIRIT. Empty yourself. Die to self. Ask to receive ALL of MY SPIRIT—humble surrender—making ME your MASTER and LORD. Without this, you are still a slave to MY enemy. He is your father and sin is your master and you work its will and do its bidding against MY Kingdom.

I am the SHEPHERD. MY sheep hear MY Voice, MY sheep know MY Voice, MY Will. MY sheep do MY Will and I will save them when I come to rescue MY own from the terrors that are coming to the earth and the rebellious who remain. Terror will strike those who remain behind, so come to ME now in full surrender. Repent of your evil done against a HOLY GOD, forgive those around you, for without forgiveness you will not enter MY Kingdom.

I am only coming for those who want to be fully in MY Will. These are MY Requirements to receive a garment that is free of stains, spots, and wrinkles.

Come now before it is too late to prepare your robe and to have the proper garment for MY Wedding Banquet. Only those dressed properly will be attending. Let ME Clothe you in humility, righteousness, and make you ready for MY Soon Coming Rescue.

The hour is near. The window of time between now and MY Approach to earth is diminishing quickly. I am giving many warnings. Very few are listening. Very few will be removed to safety. Wash your robes in MY Blood.

The hour approaches for MY Return. Darkness looms over the earth.

I am not a man that I should lie,

The EVERLASTING SAVIOR of Mankind.

John 6:70: JESUS answered them, Have not I chosen you twelve, and one of you is a devil?

Romans 3:13: Their throat is an open sepulchre; with their tongues they have used deceit; the poison of asps is under their lips:

Revelation 7:14: And I said unto him, Sir, thou knowest. And he said to me, These are they which came out of great tribulation, and have washed their robes, and made them white in the Blood of the LAMB.

John 8:44: Ye are of your father the devil, and the lusts of your father ye will do. He was a murderer from the beginning, and abode not in the truth, because there is no truth in him. When he speaketh a lie, he speaketh of his own: for he is a liar, and the father of it.

Galatians 5:9: A little leaven leaveneth the whole lump.

John 10:27: MY sheep hear MY Voice, and I know them, and they follow ME:

Numbers 23:19: GOD is not a man, that HE should lie; neither the son of man, that he should repent: hath HE said, and shall HE not do it? Or hath HE spoken, and shall HE not make it good?

OBJECT LESSON: VOTING FOR EVIL

I have been very outspoken about why Christians cannot cast a vote for evil even though so many now believe in supporting the lesser of two evils. I want to provide for you an object lesson I received from the LORD a while back:

The LORD revealed something to me through my son, who has the amazing gift of seeing into the spiritual realm. When my son was just 14, he and I went out to eat and while at the restaurant, my son felt compelled to give his Bible to a teenager who was accompanied by four adults. The four adults would not allow the youth to accept my son's Bible as they explained that they were Jehovah's Witnesses—a known anti-Christian cult. The five people sat near us at a round table and while we were eating, my startled son looked over and reported to me that he suddenly saw four large demons—

one standing behind each of the adults and a short demon standing behind the youth with his hand outstretched over the youth's head.

2 John 1:10-11 says: [10]If there come any unto you, and bring not this doctrine, receive him not into your house, neither bid him GOD speed: [11]For he that biddeth him GOD speed is partaker of his evil deeds.

With this verse in mind—it only stands to reason that you don't bring such people into your home who are practicing cultists like Jehovah's Witnesses because they are influenced directly by demons as the LORD had revealed through my son to me. The Mormon cult (they believe that the LORD's brother is Lucifer) that Mitt Romney so embraces along with Barak Obama's promotion of Islam are absolutely no different than Jehovah's Witnesses if you study them: antichrist cults. All are a far cry from the Gospel of CHRIST.

Now something else the LORD revealed to me goes back to the beginning of time, when evil entered the world and Adam and Eve ate from the Tree of the Knowledge of Good and Evil. Christians understand that Adam and Eve ate of the knowledge of evil and then evil entered the world—but what about the knowledge of good? Well the knowledge of good here is the concept that the world can do good works apart from being in GOD's Perfect Will. For example: when evil people do good and everyone embraces the good—this is not really good. It is evil men stating they can "do good" apart from GOD and that the evil world does not need the authority of that GOD over them and they can run things just fine in their own flesh without GOD. That is the knowledge of good. Genesis 2:17: [17]But of the tree of the knowledge of good and evil, thou shalt not eat of it: for in the day that thou eatest thereof thou shalt surely die.

This is exactly what the Christians are trying to embrace when they vote for Mitt Romney who is steeped in the cult of Mormonism. They want to believe that Mitt Romney can perform good through his cult foundation (demon-possessed) viewpoint of Mormonism and that as long as it appears good and moral by men's warped standards that all is well. Well all is not well with this thinking—it is just Christians turning back to the world and the traditions of men for their hope instead of turning away from evil and depending on CHRIST no matter what the circumstances.

I can't help but to recall my son's alarming word of seeing demons accompanying the Jehovah's Witnesses cultists who sat at the table near us. How can we as Christians support leadership whose agenda's are structured from evil foundations? 1 Corinthians 10:21-22:[21]Ye cannot drink the cup of the LORD, and the cup of devils: ye cannot be partakers of the LORD's Table, and of the table of devils. [22]Do we provoke the LORD to jealousy? Are we stronger than HE?

Words from the LORD regarding this voting for evil leaders:

Children, it is I, your LORD.

You have come to an impasse. You have hit a wall. You have no viable candidate. This is not by chance, it is by my design. I have created this dilemma. I want you to face up to what is happening, your world is falling apart. It is because the world has turned its back to ME even those who call themselves by MY Name. They have made love to the world and now they have to live by the consequences. This is what happens when you turn your back to GOD. You are left with no good choices. If you vote for evil you only have evil. If you believe there is a lesser of two evils you still have evil. What do you not understand about this? I am forcing you to face ME. Turn to me and lay your life at MY Feet before it is too late.

I will not take you if still cling to this world for your answers. The world is an enmity to ME. Does MY Word not speak it? Turn to the world for your answers and if you marry this world when I come back for MY bride I will not recognize you and you will be left behind. This is what I have to say to you if you do not know what to do. The answer is get on your knees before ME and prepare for MY return. This is your ALMIGHTY GOD.

Word received from the LORD 10/12 told to Susan.

The World Is Crumbling

Wed, 31 Oct 2012

The LORD's Words: "The world is crumbling. It is coming apart. I am pulling MY Hand away."

The LORD's Words for Today (Posted at www.End-Times-Prophecy.Com)

Dear Faithful Followers of CHRIST:

"Is it too late for you to be rapture ready?"

So often people write me asking about their salvation and readiness for the SOON-COMING RAPTURE—and they want to know if it is too late for them because of their past life of sin? So here are some words of comfort to all who wonder if it is too late to make it in the coming rapture:

Romans 3:9-18 says: [9]What then? Are we better than they? No, in no wise: for we have before proved both Jews and Gentiles, that they are all under sin; [10]As it is written:

There is none righteous, no, not one: ¹¹There is none that understandeth, there is none that seeketh after GOD. ¹²They are all gone out of the way, they are together become unprofitable; there is none that doeth good, no, not one.

EVERYONE HAS REJECTED GOD—but like Lydia in Acts 16:14, the LORD opened her heart:

Acts 16:14: And a certain woman named Lydia, a seller of purple, of the city of Thyatira, which worshipped GOD, heard us: whose heart the LORD opened, that she attended unto the things which were spoken of Paul.

TODAY, IF YOU ARE SEEKING GOD—YOU WOULD NOT EVEN BE SEEKING GOD IF HE WAS NOT DRAWING YOU TO HIMSELF:

In John 6:44 the LORD says: No man can come to ME, except the FATHER which hath sent ME draw him: and I will raise him up at the last day.

SO COME TO THE LORD TODAY KNOWING, IT IS NOT TOO LATE—IT'S HIS IDEA FOR YOU TO BE SAVED! REPENT OF YOUR SIN. SURRENDER YOUR ALL TO HIS OUTRAGEOUS LOVE. ASK TO RECEIVE A FULL OIL LAMP TO BE READY AND SEE TRUTH. YOUR SALVATION CAN BE SURE—EVEN TODAY!

Words of the LORD:

"The world is crumbling. It is coming apart. I am pulling MY Hand away."

(Words Received from Our LORD by Susan, October 26-27, 2012)

I am ready to give you Words:

The world is crumbling. It is coming apart. I am pulling MY Hand away. I am retreating from the earth releasing MY Hand of Protection. I am giving back to the powers that rule the earth those who refuse to follow ME. I am allowing them to be seized by MY enemy's control because the people have turned their backs to ME and hardened their hearts. They have refused to follow their LORD and continue to turn away to the world.

Soon, I am coming to the claim the wife I have earned. I paid her bridal price. I paid it all. It was a steep price. She has been worth it and I would do it all over again, but MY Blood spilt on the cross is powerful and covers all sin for sinners who repent and submit their lives in FULL to ME: FULL submission, repentance, and ask to be filled with MY HOLY SPIRIT and to exchange your life for the indwelling of MY SPIRIT.

You must know, MY children, that this world cannot be sustained by MY enemy, his ways, and by evil men running wild unchecked by a HOLY GOD. Yet this is what so many ascribe to believe. Their downfall is sure if they continue in this line of thinking.

I am ready to bring new life to all those who want it. I bring eternal life to all those who suffer from the pain and sorrow of a dying world detached from a HOLY GOD. No good can come from separating from the Love of GOD.

Your hour is short for making things right with ME. Take heed: I am not a GOD who can be trifled with. The world is promoting a brand of evil I cannot tolerate any longer.

Letter continued on October 27, 2012:

Daughter, let US continue:

Children, why do you doubt MY Words so? Why do you read MY Book and doubt it so? Can you not see MY Words coming to pass? Do you not see the world turning to evil? This is happening on all four corners of the globe. There is not a spot left on earth that has not turned away from the LIVING GOD—all reject ME. I have been rejected in the understanding of MY Truth, MY Teachings, and MY Ways.

The people reject ME because they love their flesh. They want to appease their flesh and their carnal ways against MY Word that says: repent, forgive, submit wholly to your LORD, and die to self fully. This goes against their worldly desires. They won't have Truth and they have stopped their ears from listening to true teachings from MY HOLY SPIRIT. HE alone teaches Truth. This Truth can only come by a COMPLETE FILLING of MY SPIRIT which can only be had by a FULL SURRENDER to ME, your SAVIOR.

Once you SURRENDER your ALL to ME and make ME your COMPLETE LORD and MASTER and ask to receive MY SPIRIT in your heart FULLY then MY SPIRIT will indwell you and direct your ways and lead you to all Truth and understanding of MY Ways and MY Will for your life. Until this happens, you are lukewarm, partially filled, or empty of MY SPIRIT and your understanding of MY Word and Truth will be compromised. You will receive the teaching of men, who themselves are outside of MY Will and your understanding of MY Word will be incorrect. Only MY HOLY SPIRIT when received in ALL HIS FULLNESS in your life can give you the exact interpretation of MY Word and Truth. Only then will you understand MY Word and be able to apply it effectively to your life. This requires a FULL SURRENDER and a DEATH TO YOUR FLESH.

You must choose to want this for yourself—only you can decide. No one else can do it for you. Just as you will stand alone at MY Judgment Seat, so are you responsible for your own salvation. Decide today: will you come to ME and be MY Own or will you reject ME? This choice is yours to make. Choose this day who you will serve—the LIVING GOD or the enemy of GOD and death everlasting.

The hour approaches for MY Return. Who will you belong to when I make MY Appearance to receive MY bride and usher her out to safety?

I await your answer,

The LIVING GOD.

GOD of the LIVING.

Luke 20:38: For HE is not a GOD of the dead, but of the living: for all live unto HIM.

Ephesians 6:12: For we wrestle not against flesh and blood, but against principalities, against powers, against the rulers of the darkness of this world, against spiritual wickedness in high places.

John 12:31: Now is the judgment of this world: now shall the prince of this world be cast out.

John 12:40: HE hath blinded their eyes, and hardened their heart; that they should not see with their eyes, nor understand with their heart, and be converted, and I should heal them.

Romans 8:6: For to be carnally minded is death; but to be SPIRITUALLY minded is life and peace.

Luke 14:27: And whosoever doth not bear his cross, and come after ME, cannot be MY disciple.

1 Corinthians 2:10-13: [10]But GOD hath revealed them unto us by HIS SPIRIT: for the SPIRIT searcheth all things, yea, the deep things of GOD. [11]For what man knoweth the things of a man, save the spirit of man which is in him? Even so the things of GOD knoweth no man, but the SPIRIT of GOD. [12]Now we have received, not the spirit of the world, but the SPIRIT which is of GOD; that we might know the things that are freely given to us of GOD. [13]Which things also we speak, not in the words which man's wisdom teacheth, but which the HOLY GHOST teacheth; comparing SPIRITUAL things with SPIRITUAL.

Romans 14:10: But why dost thou judge thy brother? Or why dost thou set at nought thy brother? For we shall all stand before the judgment seat of CHRIST.

Philippians 2:12: Wherefore, my beloved, as ye have always obeyed, not as in my presence only, but now much more in my absence, work out your own salvation with fear and trembling.

Instructions on how the HOLY SPIRIT Teaches: http://www.takehisheart.com/holyspiritspiritualthings.htm

Dear Susan Davis, my name is Andre Kofi Akyere from Christian Palace International Ministries in Florida, USA. I had a vision by night about the end times that I am led to send it to you for interpretation and to warn America.

October 26th 2012, I had a vision by night, I was standing between heaven and earth above the map of America. I saw a cloud and in the midst of the cloud was consuming fire and the cloud open and fire began to destroy the west coast of America and on the east coast, floods begin to flood the land. There were three main spirits from the water and I saw myself back on the land fighting them at their camps. The LORD gave me Jeremiah 25:15-22: THE VOICE OF THE LORD came to me saying this is MY wrath and judgment. They need to repent from serious sexual immorality.

Susan received this confirmation for this word from Donna McDonald, October 30, 2012, who also hears from the LORD: Yes MY daughter, I have words for you regarding this brother and his prophecy:

These words are true. Fire will consume the west coast and water the east coast. There will be fire and water like no other. Please take heed to the warning and get right with me. Repent and move towards me like a runaway freight train with reckless abandon. This is your LORD and SAVIOR, YAHUSHUA, Amen

Sun, 4 Nov 2012

The LORD's Words: "This Country has turned its back to ME."

The LORD's Words for Today (Posted at www.End-Times-Prophecy.Com)

Dear Faithful Followers of CHRIST:

The new slogan for this campaign in the U.S. for many Christians is "Vote for the Lesser of Two Evils." Now there are two main categories—one who has been the most unbiblical President on record and the second, a candidate who has a long-running history of being steeped in an anti-Christian cult—a cult that embraces the idea that our LORD is brother to Lucifer (satan), I want to add.

Perhaps the trouble with this situation is that the Christians who feel they should vote for the "lesser of two evils" are just too close to the situation. They seem to think that what is happening here is about two people: Barack Obama and Mitt Romney—when it is so much more than that—it is about a culture that has become so evil and counter-CHRIST that the culture has TOTALLY chosen anti-GOD leadership to rule over itself.

So many believe that it is better to have the lesser of two evils over them to support the thing they have chosen above GOD HIMSELF: their pagan god and idol "AMERICA." America, the pagan god and idol of many now represents evil and anti-GOD philosophies and way of life: pornography; sexual immorality; disregarding and blaspheming GOD; antichrist views; materialism at all cost; the occult and satan worship; and new age philosophies.

America is the representation of its true leadership: satan. How do we know? We can know by their fruit: turn on the TV; go to the movies; go to the bookstores; listen to the news; and go to the mega-churches who embrace prosperity but reject the presence of the HOLY SPIRIT.

Mitt Romney is the alternative to Barack Obama—which seems to appease so many Christians because he looks so upright. However, Romney is putting out a brand of evil as dangerous as his opponent: the kind of evil that is not easily spotted because it looks so right. Romney is just like the Pharisees of the LORD's time. They seemed so law abiding, upright, and representative of GOD—but the LORD took exception to this when he called them White Washed Tombs. That is the way it is with Romney and his Mormon cult—White Washed Tombs.

Many who are deceived say they are not voting for their church leadership so why not vote for Mitt Romney and his pagan background to run the country? No you aren't voting for church leaders—just someone who oversees nuclear weapons and control over the military—that's all. Plain and simple—you vote for either of these candidates—both EVIL in their own way—and you are casting a vote AGAINST GOD no matter how you slice it or try to talk yourself into feeling good about it.

The United States is being dealt the hand it deserves. When you become a culture so flooded with evil then how can you expect GOD to turn around and reward that culture with the blessings HE has so abundantly given this country in the past? GOD is very clear in the Bible the outcome of rejecting HIS Will. And do we really want GOD to reward this evil we as a culture have descended to? That would go against WHO GOD is and what HE represents. And GOD clearly won't reward evil.

Matthew 23:27-28: [27] Woe unto you, scribes and Pharisees, hypocrites! For ye are like unto whited sepulchres, which indeed appear beautiful outward, but are within full of dead men's bones, and of all uncleanness. [28] Even so ye also outwardly appear righteous unto men, but within ye are full of hypocrisy and iniquity.

Prophetic words 10/25/12 to Susan D. from the LORD at 11:44am:

I will release MY Mighty Hand over the U.S. They will not rebound from the evil they have brought on themselves. This country has turned its back to ME. A stench and stink has risen to my throne room. This country believes it can be revived but it has sunk too far down and now it will face my judgment. Judgment is coming to this land that once called on MY Name in truth and liberty. These people have now rushed into the arms of evil and have desired wickedness and rebellion in place of MY Glory and Truth. I will deliver destruction and only MY bride will escape. Only she will be brought out to safety. Destruction is coming to this land that once loved GOD and now loves evil in all forms. MY Word bears witness to these words.

Prophetic words 10/25/12 to Susan D. from the Lord at 1:25pm:

Yes, the culture has moved away from my bride. She is left standing alone in a field of wolves. She is singularly still following ME, while everyone around her is still going after evil. If they want to embrace evil so badly they are pulling away from MY Truth. They can't have evil and ME both. We are in the days where the good will be called bad and the bad will be called good. If they pursue evil they are not MY bride. MY bride's discernment comes straight from the HOLY SPIRIT.

Prophetic words 10/27/25 to Donna M. at 1:52am:

Yes, my daughter, I have words regarding the messages above. They are my words and I want you to put them out on email for all to see especially those of MY bride, MY chosen ones who believe they are to vote in this evil election. Evil plus evil begets evil. It is a lose-lose for MY bride. If she votes in this election, I cannot call her MY bride. This is MY Truth and you can bank on it. YAHUSHUA, GOD ALMIGHTY Amen.

Words from the Lord to Susan D. 10/27/12 4:07pm

Lord, what happens if the bride votes in the election?

My daughter, Susan, I am ready to give words to you. These are the words:

The bride is not to waste her time in such activities. This is such a waste of time. The bride cannot vote for evil in any form. If she supports evil she only gets evil. There will only be evil reaped through these two candidates. They hotly stand against ME. One looks better than the other but this is by design of MY enemy. He comes as an angel of light, by deception. It looks good but it is still evil. Any alteration of MY Word and Truth is a corruption of its original meaning. This candidate stands for lies and corruption of MY Truth. The people are deceived because he looks so right to them. THERE IS NOTHING RIGHT ABOUT THIS WARPED RELIGION THAT HE HAILS FROM. IT IS A BASTARDIZATION OF MY TRUTH. MY BRIDE CANNOT VOTE FOR LIES AND DECEPTION. SHE EITHER STANDS WITH ME, OR THE WORLD. THIS IS WHERE THE LINE IS DRAWN NOW. All things are changed because the world has become so evil. There are very few who pursue MY Truth. Most are clinging to the world and are lost. These are MY Words and they are solid.

Words of the LORD:

"I am that GATE—I am the NARROW PATH, the WAY OUT."

(Words Received from Our LORD by Susan, November 1, 2012)

Daughter, listen closely:

There are many dark clouds arising in the world. They are gathering around MY children: those who follow ME with a passion.

I am watching out for MY own. I am a GOD WHO is true to MY Word. I will protect MY bride. She cannot be touched by MY enemy—as long as she is FULLY MINE and pressing into ME. He cannot take her soul away. Her soul is MINE for eternity and MY

SPIRIT guards her spirit. OUR SPIRITS are ONE: MY wife and I. This is by design—an eternal plan forged at the foundation of the world and no one can pluck MY true bride out of MY Hand.

She has her footing on the Solid ROCK—I am that ROCK. I am the source of all peace, security, safety, and well-being. Only I deliver a foundation of wholeness. I bring serenity and peace of mind in the midst of the storm. I calm the raging seas of the heart. I am the Great REDEEMER and COMFORTER. All is well when you are under MY Care and Keeping: all else is sinking sand and shifting shadows.

The times are too hard to go it alone. MY enemy lurks around you like a prowling lion looking for who he can pursue and destroy. Only those who rest safely in the center of MY Will, finds safety. In MY Will, all who find rest there find the salvation of their soul, right standing with GOD, and resilience against the waves that rage around them in a world of human turmoil. Only through MY peace of mind, which I give freely to those who seek ME, will the world seem navigatable.

Children, you must come toward ME now—you must run into MY Open Arms. Come swiftly, like an elk freed from a trap. Run to your freedom. I am that GATE—I am the NARROW PATH, the WAY OUT. Only by ME can you find freedom…only by MY Blood. All other doors lead to hell. Many are in hell because they did not seek ME.

Come and find salvation for your hungry soul. Let ME give water for your thirsty spirit. Let ME bring healing to your mind and your heart. Only the waves of MY Love rolling over you will carry you. MY Love is a banquet set before you to taste and enjoy. MY enemy may offer you what tastes sweet at first, but it will soon become bitter poison leading to your death.

Seek ME for all your answers. Flee from the trap set for you by MY enemy. He knows the hour is short and he is bent on your destruction. Save yourself in MY Blood Covering that I alone can give you to shield you from the judgment deserved for your life of sin against the Will of a HOLY GOD. Only the ransom I paid for you on a hard cross of death will cover your sin-debt due when you come face-to-face with your GOD: JUDGE SUPREME of the Universe. MY Holy Name will be vindicated for all those who rise up against ME with unrepentant hearts who will not acknowledge and receive MY Debt paid in full for them. Shock and dismay will be their reaction when they face their GOD on that day that they render an account of their life.

All will stand before ME and give an account of their life. MY bride will receive her glory and honor and MY enemies will receive death and eternal destruction.

How do you choose?

Honor ME and humble yourself. SURRENDER ALL to ME; REPENT for a life of sin; FORGIVE all those around you; INVITE MY SPIRIT to take over your life giving HIM FULL ACCESS, holding nothing back. Come to ME now. Your time is slipping away. MY Warnings are sure.

This is your GOD.

The LOVER of your soul…SAVIOR of all mankind.

John 10:27-30: [27]MY sheep hear MY Voice, and I know them, and they follow ME: [28]And I give unto them eternal life; and they shall never perish, neither shall any man pluck them out of MY Hand. ²⁹MY FATHER, which gave them ME, is Greater than all; and no man is able to pluck them out of MY FATHER's Hand. ³⁰I and MY FATHER are ONE.

Matthew 7:25-27: ²⁵And the rain descended, and the floods came, and the winds blew, and beat upon that house; and it fell not: for it was founded upon a rock. ²⁶And every one that heareth these sayings of mine, and doeth them not, shall be likened unto a foolish man, which built his house upon the sand: ²⁷And the rain descended, and the floods came, and the winds blew, and beat upon that house; and it fell: and great was the fall of it.

Psalm 116:7: Return unto thy rest, O my soul; for the LORD hath dealt bountifully with thee.

Matthew 7:14: Because strait is the gate, and narrow is the way, which leadeth unto life, and few there be that find it.

John 4:13-14: ¹³JESUS answered and said unto her, Whosoever drinketh of this water shall thirst again: ¹⁴But whosoever drinketh of the water that I shall give him shall never thirst; but the water that I shall give him shall be in him a well of water springing up into everlasting life.

Psalm 119:103: How sweet are THY Words unto my taste! Yea, sweeter than honey to my mouth!

Revelation 20:12: And I saw the dead, small and great, stand before GOD; and the books were opened: and another book was opened, which is the Book of Life: and the dead were judged out of those things which were written in the books, according to their works.

Have you been baptized in the HOLY SPIRIT?

Did you know the baptism of the HOLY SPIRIT is different than the water baptism?

Matthew 3:11: (John the Baptist) I indeed baptize you with water unto repentance, but HE that cometh after me is mightier than I, whose shoes I am not worthy to bear: HE shall baptize you with the HOLY GHOST, and with fire:

Acts 10:44-48: [44]While Peter yet spake these words, the HOLY GHOST fell on all them (Cornelius and family) which heard the word. [45]And they of the circumcision which believed were astonished, as many as came with Peter, because that on the Gentiles also was poured out the gift (baptism) of the HOLY GHOST. [46]For they heard them speak with tongues, and magnify GOD. Then answered Peter, [47]Can any man forbid water (water baptism—a separate baptism), that these should not be baptized, which have received the HOLY GHOST as well as we? [48]And he commanded them to be baptized in the name of the LORD (in water as well as the HOLY SPIRIT Baptism they received from the HOLY SPIRIT). Then prayed they him to tarry certain days.

(Words Received from Our LORD by Susan, May 4, 2012)

Only I give the Power you need to keep you in MY Will. The flesh cannot succeed at staying in the Will of GOD. Only by MY Power is any man successful in walking in MY Will—flesh cannot accomplish this task. It is the Power of the HOLY SPIRIT.

A partial surrender does not allot the fullness of MY SPIRIT to bring the individual under the controlling Power of MY SPIRIT thus they cannot successfully ward off evil, sin, and be in MY Will. They are considered "lukewarm" and lost. Partial surrender is not "surrender."

Make no mistake; a partial surrender leads to death the same as an outright denial of ME as GOD.

Repentance is "key" to the person's surrender. If they are still believing they have no sin or they don't need forgiveness how can they be freed by the evil that still controls them?

Remorse over sin is the beginning of healing—healing heart, soul, spirit—all is interrelated. A repentant heart, a humble heart, can receive the salvation of their soul and will enter MY Kingdom upon receiving the HOLY SPIRIT by baptism.

This is part of releasing the person into freedom to be freed of demonic spirits: true remorse over past sin, acknowledgement of sin before a HOLY GOD and then the filling of MY SPIRIT and total submission to MY Ways and to ME as the individual's LORD and MASTER.

All other expressions are weak and ineffectual. The person must be submitted to ME completely to be relieved of the power of MY enemy and I must be their undisputed MASTER so that the individual can be walking in MY Will conquering sin and filled with the Power of MY SPIRIT. Not before will the individual be able to deal successfully with vanquishing sin in their lives. This is the "narrow path." All other paths lead to destruction.

Deuteronomy 30:19: I call heaven and earth to record this day against you, that I have set before you life and death, blessing and cursing: therefore choose life that both thou and thy seed may live:

Your Lamp Oil Filled? The LORD will take only those 'sold out' to HIM and filled with the HOLY SPIRIT in the coming rapture of the church (remember, only the five virgins with full oil lamps are ready when the Bridegroom comes). If you don't think you are 'sold out' to HIM because you are caught up in things of this world then there is still time if you engage yourself right now in a relentless pursuit of knowing and following HIM. You must first be filled, 'baptized' with the HOLY SPIRIT.

You can be baptized in the HOLY SPIRIT right now: you can pray this suggested prayer: "In the LORD's Name, I pray to be baptized in the Names of the FATHER, the SON, and the HOLY SPIRIT. I pray to be filled up completely from the top of my head to the bottom of my toes. I pray for my Spiritual eyes to be opened and for the scales to fall off and I pray for a bolder testimony for the LORD JESUS and for MY OIL LAMP TO BE FILLED TO THE TOP. I surrender my ALL to the LORD and repent for all my sins from a sincere heart of remorse for these things done before a HOLY GOD." (You can also be prayed over by someone who has been baptized in the HOLY SPIRIT.)

You don't have to go anywhere or do anything as it has to do with the attitude of your heart. Just pray and you will receive through a sincere heart. Surrender your life over completely and repent from all your sins to the LORD. If you desire to be baptized in the HOLY SPIRIT, stop right now, where you are and pray. You can pray the suggested prayer above. You have ABSOLUTELY NOTHING TO LOSE AND EVERYTHING TO GAIN! When you pray to receive then 'press in' and read your bible or do it more and pray more. Fasting also is recommended because it is by fasting from food, a meal, or something enjoyed such as your iPod, TV/movies, worldly pursuits, whatever we do that we 'die to our flesh.'

Fasting does not replace salvation by JESUS' Blood at all. It just means we are dying to our flesh which is pleasing to the LORD for greater personal intimacy, seeking answers through prayers, whereas salvation is a free gift from GOD and not earned by any human act of sacrifice. These are verses that support a second baptism (the other being water baptism—the water baptism can come before or after the HOLY SPIRIT baptism) given from the HOLY SPIRIT:

Matthew 3:11: "As for me, I baptize you with water for repentance, but HE WHO is coming after me is mightier than I, and I am not fit to remove HIS sandals; HE will baptize you with the HOLY SPIRIT and fire."

Mark 1:8: "I baptized you with water; but HE will baptize you with the HOLY SPIRIT."

Luke 3:16: "John answered and said to them all, 'As for me, I baptize you with water; but ONE is coming WHO is mightier than I, and I am not fit to untie the thong of HIS sandals; HE will baptize you with the HOLY SPIRIT and fire."

John 1:33: "And I did not recognize HIM, but HE WHO sent me to baptize in water said to me, "HE upon WHOM you see the SPIRIT descending and remaining upon HIM, this is the ONE WHO baptizes in the HOLY SPIRIT."

Acts 1:5: "For John baptized with water, but you shall be baptized with the HOLY SPIRIT not many days from now."

Acts 11:15-16: " [15]And as I began to speak, the Holy Ghost fell on them, as on us at the beginning. And I remembered the Word of the LORD, how HE used to say, 'John baptized with water, but you shall be baptized with the HOLY SPIRIT.'"

Free End Times Prophetic Books from Deborah Melissa:

The books can be downloaded for FREE: http://end-times-prophecy.com/blog/?p=2836

Book 1: 'The Final Call' - The book is about the Bride and what the LORD says about the Bride.
www.smashwords.com/books/view/118164

Book 2: 'The Exodus' - The book is about coming out of Egypt and how to get into the Promised Land (Millennium).
www.smashwords.com/books/view/118176

Book 3: 'My Son David' - The book is about the "rulers and reigners" in the Millennium. Those who will rule and reign with CHRIST.
www.smashwords.com/books/view/118181

Sun, 11 Nov 2012

The LORD's Words: "I can only offer the Keys to MY Kingdom. I cannot force them into your hands."

The LORD's Words for Today (Posted at www.End-Times-Prophecy.Com)

Dear Faithful Followers of CHRIST:

After I began to hear from the LORD all through the day, the LORD gave me a brief "Jonah" lesson on obeying GOD. I was at my mother's assisted living at the time and I was heading to the elevator of her building to run out and pick up my son from school and I was running late. There was an older woman in the lobby area by the elevator and the LORD told me to give her a word from HIM.

Wow can you believe it, I told the LORD I was late to pick up my son and I could not do it.

Then the LORD said very calmly to me: "I give you permission to go, daughter."

Well the next thing that happened was astounding. As I stepped onto the elevator, the woman across the room from the elevator who I was supposed to talk (but didn't) immediately jumped up from her chair and dashed across the room making a beeline straight for the elevator before the door shut. This woman was standing right next to me on the elevator and with my eyes popping out of my head, I said to the LORD, "I guess you want me to talk to her," to which HE then said, "Yes" and HE gave me a word for this lady which was very meaningful to her.

That day, I learned a lesson just as Jonah, who ran from GOD, had learned only to find himself in the belly of a whale. The lesson is to obey GOD when HE tells you to do something. Just like these letters I put out for the LORD, I receive a lot of grief about them—but that doesn't mean I can disobey GOD, no matter what people say or think.

"Mark of the Beast"

Now, I want to talk about the things the LORD has revealed to me to share with you. I want to talk about the "mark of the beast"—it is the RFID Chip according to the LORD despite what many people—even what many ministry people say. Most people want to debunk the truth that the current microchip is the mark of the beast because they don't like the idea that the LORD's Coming could be so soon and that puts us right at the door of HIS coming if the RFID chip is in fact the mark of the beast. The RFID chip (also available as a "mark" now) lines up with the bible's description of it exactly: it is to be placed in the forehead or the right hand just as the RFID chip and it is usable in for buying and selling.

Nowhere in the bible does it say that this will be a second or third generation of the mark that matches the bible's description as so many are saying that the RFID chip is only the "forerunner" to the actual mark—this is a lie.

Revelation 13:17: And that no man might buy or sell, save he that had the mark, or the name of the beast, or the number of his name.

The LORD showed me that the RFID chip is the "mark of the beast" by revealing to me that everything is bar coded now and that means this chip works with this coding and the bar coding is being established everywhere (the military, healthcare venues, and retail venues) to accommodate the one and only "mark." This is why it is wrong, even evil to make people believe that this chip is okay to take.

I want to ask these ministry people who think it is okay to spread these lies—just who gave you permission to put other people's eternal salvation at risk by telling them falsely that this chip is okay and probably not the mark of the beast when it meets every criteria in the bible perfectly for the mark? Already thousands even possibly millions of people have been chipped.

Now, I want to go on to reveal something else to you very powerful the LORD has shown me about this RFID "mark." Watch this youtube about this miraculous dream revelation from GOD about the "mark of the beast" and President Obama's initiation of the chip: http://www.youtube.com/watch?v=lcLqHcl8M20

Now ONLY BECAUSE OF THIS DREAM REVELATION PROVIDED BY GOD HIMSELF—it led to the following chart/link: http://www.federalnewsradio.com/pdfs/cisco_federal_healthcare.pdf
In this Obamacare chart, you can see a military man going through a hospital and at various stations you can see this military patient receiving assistance by way of the records on his RFID microchip (notice the chart uses a military personnel to showcase this technology—you can see more about the military plan to microchip their personnel here in this article: http://www.mobiledia.com/news/134354.html). Ultimately he is at home and is able to be checked remotely via his RFID microchip. This chart has the Obama logo/seal on it and is part of the Obama Health Care plan; the same in which Obama mocked GOD suggesting "that the ground didn't open up" the day the bill passed with the microchip component that was squirreled deep within its 2,000-page document.

Something amazing the LORD showed me was in the three little words in the bible "HE CAUSETH ALL." This is incredible—it is the Obamacare program that puts forth the proclamation and legal right that the microchip can/will be utilized for human tracking—so it is the Obama initiative that we see the "mark of the beast" initially surfacing—HE CAUSETH ALL—he initiates it—he is causing it.

To understand what the bible is saying here, let us look at the standard definition of the verb "cause" which means: to make something happen, usually something bad. To date, there is no one else whose name is attached to this initiative the way the Obamacare program and the current US administration is:

Revelation 13:16: And he causeth all, both small and great, rich and poor, free and bond, to receive a mark in their right hand, or in their foreheads:

Also, don't let secular views and speculation about when this technology might be forced on people dictate your opinion/thinking on when you need to get ready for the LORD's return. GOD is ultimately in charge and the rapture will occur first forcing the use of the microchip to the forefront to bring the world back under submission to the antichrist.

So now is the time to watch for the rapture to occur since the onset of the chip by human time tables is growing extremely close. It is absolutely time to get serious about watching for the LORD's return and to debunk all the false information that indicates otherwise put out for the purpose of damning people to hell by satan himself.

4. Calamity Will Reach An Unheard Of Plateau

Words of the LORD:

"Seek MY Truth; pray for eyes to see the Truth; and what is soon approaching the world—unbridled evil."

Words Received from Our LORD by Susan, November 7, 2012

Yes WE can begin:

Here are MY Words. They are for MY children:

Children, I want you to listen to MY Words. I am a GOD of Truth—Everlasting Truth. I have stated to you the direction that I am moving in. I am trying to wake you, MY children up!

Can you see the dark hour that is approaching? It is moving fast to the hour of MY Return. I am a GOD WHO makes promises and keeps them. I am True to MY Word. MY Word will come about as I have said them. Read and study MY Book.

Soon children, I will allow the worst calamity to strike this earth that mankind has ever witnessed. It will be disaster upon disaster.

At the point MY bride is removed, the calamity will reach an unheard of plateau and those left behind will have unrivaled regrets realizing what they are about to face. No one will escape the hand of MY enemy—who claims to know ME as their SAVIOR. All will be wounded and pierced for aligning with ME against MY enemy. The destruction of those who love ME will be certain. There will be no one who will escape the evil intended for those who claim to be MY own after the bride has been lifted out to safety—better to know ME now and to be part of MY bride.

This can be yours if you will just LAY DOWN YOUR LIFE and SURRENDER YOUR ALL to ME. Give ME your FULL COMMITMENT. CHOOSE FOR ME against the world and all she stands for. REPENT of your sin you have committed while in the world. FORGIVE those around you. Ask for a FILLING of MY HOLY SPIRIT. SEEK TO FIND ME THROUGH MY BOOK. PROCLAIM YOUR DECISION TO OTHERS and tell others about the love you know through MY Sacrifice.

In exchange, I will give you Everlasting Life. I will write your name in MY Book of Life. I will give you a new name and a new mind and MY SPIRIT will indwell your spirit and you will be sealed by MY HOLY SPIRIT. There is very little time remaining to come to ME now. You don't want to delay as evil is moving over the land in rapid succession. The hour of your redemption is nigh if you are among MY bride.

Come, let US reason together: seek MY Truth; pray for eyes to see the Truth; and what is soon approaching the world—unbridled evil. Dark storm clouds are forming. Don't be caught unawares in the trap of MY enemy who longs to destroy MY children.

This Word is for your benefit. Don't mock and reject it. Turn to your only hope.

Your SAVIOR,

CHRIST the LORD.

Isaiah 45:7:I form the light, and create darkness: I make peace, and create evil: I the LORD do all these things.

Deuteronomy 32:4: HE is the ROCK, HIS work is perfect: for all HIS ways are judgment: a GOD of truth and without iniquity, just and right is HE.

Mark 13:20: And except that the LORD had shortened those days, no flesh should be saved: but for the elect's sake, whom HE hath chosen, HE hath shortened the days.

Revelation 20:4: And I saw thrones, and they sat upon them, and judgment was given unto them: and I saw the souls of them that were beheaded for the witness of JESUS, and for the Word of GOD, and which had not worshipped the beast, neither his image, neither had received his mark upon their foreheads, or in their hands; and they lived and reigned with CHRIST a thousand years.

Revelation 3:5: He that overcometh, the same shall be clothed in white raiment; and I will not blot out his name out of the Book of Life, but I will confess his name before MY FATHER, and before HIS angels.

Revelation 2:17: He that hath an ear, let him hear what the SPIRIT saith unto the churches; To him that overcometh will I give to eat of the hidden manna, and will give him a white stone, and in the stone a new name written, which no man knoweth saving he that receiveth it.

Romans 12:2: And be not conformed to this world: but be ye transformed by the renewing of your mind, that ye may prove what is that good, and acceptable, and perfect, will of GOD.

Ephesians 1:13: In whom ye also trusted, after that ye heard the word of truth, the gospel of your salvation: in whom also after that ye believed, ye were sealed with that HOLY SPIRIT of promise,

Words of the LORD:

"I can only offer the keys to MY Kingdom—I cannot force them into your hands."

(Words Received from Our LORD by Susan, November 9, 2012)

Children, it is I your LORD. I want to speak to you now.

There is a time coming where I will send a blast from MY Nostril down to this earth of MY Wrath and indignation against evil men—men who reject their GOD. The world has become an offense to MY Holy Senses. I no longer take pleasure in it. I find no pleasure in looking upon it. Only MY bride is pleasing to ME—a small select few who pursue ME at all cost. These are the ones I will soon release from the tyranny about to take over the earth.

MY precious bride will be unscathed and preserved from the evil overtaking this world. I cannot stand by and allow this world to wallow in its depravity unchecked any further. Soon there will be full retribution for the choices men make against a Holy GOD—their CREATOR—RULER SUPREME.

Although men choose not to believe in ME, that does not change the fact that I exist and all will face ME—each to give an account of his life before MY Holy Face to come into MY Eternal Glory by MY Blood Covering and Free Salvation or to face death, destruction, eternal punishment.

There will only be two possibilities for the outcome of your soul on the day you face your GOD and stand before ME to face the judgment of your life of decisions: either for ME or against ME. This will be the conclusion of your life on earth to receive eternal salvation and rest for your soul in MY Heavenlies or to receive the reward of punishment for rejecting the Will of GOD for your life.

So many stand before ME at the climax of their life on earth completely unprepared to face ME and are horrified at the outcome of their lifetime of choosing against ME when they find themselves outside MY Kingdom for all eternity. Very few choose the narrow path that leads to the eternal preservation of their soul. The enemy's deception runs deep and wide: and broad is the road to destruction. Few make their way down MY Narrow Way of Salvation.

Most do not want to pay the price for MY Free Salvation. I, YEHUSHUA, paid the price for the salvation of men and in turn few are willing to give up the world, surrender their all, exchange their will for MY Will, carry their cross. Only a handful discover that what looks the hardest is ultimately the easiest way to go in the long run. Few persevere and overcome their fears of—and desires for the ways of—this lost world.

I can only offer the keys to MY Kingdom—I cannot force them into your hands. You must want to be freed from your attraction for this evil world and the lusts thereof. Only you can choose for yourself— no one else. Though many may try to reach you, only you must decide for or against ME.

You only have a short time remaining to run under MY Blood Covering to safety to pursue ME in all your ways and to surrender your all to ME with a remorseful repentant heart, forgiving all those around you. MY Word is complete. Don't waste your time with the words of men. Seek MY True Word for the cleansing of your heart.

Purify your soul with a complete filling of MY SPIRIT within your spirit. Let MY SPIRIT burn out your impurities and make you whole and perfect to come before your GOD in this final hour. Choose the righteous path; turn from evil.

MY Love can sustain you in this life and prepare you for the Glories of the next life in MY Soon Coming Kingdom. Come and be fitted for your royal robes—white and pure.

I am the HOT COAL to purify your lips*

Come into MY Purifying Fires

Luke 21:36: Watch ye therefore, and pray always, that ye may be accounted worthy to escape all these things that shall come to pass, and to stand before the SON of man.

Romans 14:12: So then every one of us shall give account of himself to GOD.

Romans 12:2: And be not conformed to this world: but be ye transformed by the renewing of your mind, that ye may prove what is that good, and acceptable, and perfect, Will of GOD.

Matthew 7:13: Enter ye in at the strait gate: for wide is the gate, and broad is the way, that leadeth to destruction, and many there be which go in thereat:

Luke 14:27: And whosoever doth not bear his cross, and come after ME, cannot be MY disciple.

Matthew 11:30:For MY Yoke is easy, and MY Burden is light.

*Isaiah 6:5-7: [5] Then said I, Woe is me! For I am undone; because I am a man of unclean lips, and I dwell in the midst of a people of unclean lips: for mine eyes have seen the KING, the LORD of hosts.

⁶ Then flew one of the seraphims unto me, having a live coal in his hand, which he had taken with the tongs from off the altar: ⁷ And he laid it upon my mouth, and said, Lo, this hath touched thy lips; and thine iniquity is taken away, and thy sin purged.

Sun, 18 Nov 2012

The LORD's Words: "Those who will be left behind will become sober quickly"

The LORD's Words for Today (Posted at www.End-Times-Prophecy.Com)

Dear Faithful Followers of CHRIST:

During the recent US presidential election, the Christians were perplexed about the backgrounds of the two candidates: one, the most unbiblical president in recorded history and the other, a strong follower of an anti-Christian cult. Many Christians even placated themselves by believing that voting for the LESSER OF TWO EVILS was a decision that was ordained by GOD and their duty as followers of CHRIST. Choosing for evil is never promoted by GOD. Now the truth is: of two evils—evil is still in power (and would have been no matter how the election would have been concluded).

Christians scratch their heads and wonder where is GOD when all this is happening? Did GOD take a vacation while the US elections took place? Let's take a look at the following scriptures from the bible:

Judges 3:12: And the children of Israel did evil again in the sight of the LORD: and the LORD strengthened Eglon the king of Moab against Israel, because they had done evil in the Sight of the LORD.

Judges 6:1: And the children of Israel did evil in the sight of the LORD: and the LORD delivered them into the hand of Midian seven years.

Ezra 1:1: Now in the first year of Cyrus king of Persia, that the word of the LORD by the mouth of Jeremiah might be fulfilled, the LORD stirred up the spirit of Cyrus king of Persia, that he made a proclamation throughout all his kingdom, and put it also in writing.

Exodus 10:1: And the LORD said unto Moses, Go in unto Pharaoh: for I have hardened his heart, and the heart of his servants, that I might shew these MY Signs before him:

John 19:10-11:[10] Then saith Pilate unto HIM, Speakest thou not unto me? Knowest THOU not that I have power to crucify THEE, and have power to release THEE? [11]JESUS answered, Thou couldest have no power at all against ME, except it were given thee from above: therefore he that delivered ME unto thee hath the greater sin.

John 12:40: HE hath blinded their eyes, and hardened their heart; that they should not see with their eyes, nor understand with their heart, and be converted, and I should heal them.

Romans 11:8: (According as it is written, GOD hath given them the spirit of slumber, eyes that they should not see, and ears that they should not hear;) unto this day.

Revelation 17:17: For GOD hath put in their hearts to fulfil HIS Will, and to agree, and give their kingdom unto the beast, until the Words of GOD shall be fulfilled.

GOD IS NEVER ON VACATION. HE IS ALWAYS IN CHARGE even when people think otherwise. So what is going on?

GOD is delivering to the Americans (and the world) what they want—an evil leader in exchange for their evil choices, pagan beliefs, anti-GOD desires. How do Christians expect GOD to reward a grossly evil culture with moral leadership? This world is only reaping the harvest of what it plants everyday through choices against CHRIST and GOD's Will.

Now that GOD has allowed evil leadership to move into the White House (and around the world) it is clear that this overwhelming evil cannot be turned around apart from the power of GOD. GOD is not going to reward the all-consuming evil that has overtaken the world. HE is going to allow evil to have its way and to take over this sinking world to punish humanity for its crimes against a HOLY GOD.

Christians: your hope does not lie in your immoral governments; in your unreliable economies; in your lukewarm church leadership; in your humanistic pursuits; and in your own personal will and goals. YOU HAVE ONE DOOR TO SAFETY: OUR LORD and SAVIOR CHRIST. There are NO OTHER ANSWERS no matter how hard you search or no matter how you try to convince yourself otherwise. This is what GOD is trying to show everyone: that there is no other place to turn now except to HIM. SURRENDER YOUR ALL to HIM today. Don't waste one more second living outside the Will of GOD. Who knows that it may be more than your own life you are saving if you turn your life over to CHRIST?

Words of the LORD:

"Those who will be left behind will become sober quickly after they learn the error of their ways and the tyranny they are about to face."

Words Received from Our LORD by Susan, November 13, 2012.

November 13, 2012

WE May Begin:

MY children, it is your LORD of lords speaking. I am your Great GOD, Sovereign LORD, RULER of all.

The world no longer takes its GOD seriously. It wants to be ruled by evil—evil has come in and taken over. This is by MY design. I have allowed it because the people have chosen against ME in their hearts. They have chosen the lust for the world over their GOD, so now they will have their way and what results from rejecting GOD SUPREME for the lusts of the world.

Soon they shall find out what it means to distance yourself from GOD to pursue false gods, pagan beliefs, and the love of the flesh. This transparent, empty worship for things that have no worth will soon turn against all who partake in it. Their pursuit of the empty and worthless will lead them to great loss and eternal consequences: eternal punishment.

I do not take lightly to those who reject ME. The outcome will be very bad for those who choose against ME for the wooden idols and love of mammon. These will be left behind to face the worst. Very soon this will play out. Those who will be left behind will become sober quickly after they learn the error of their ways and the tyranny they are about to face. They will have missed their escape and salvation from tribulation and their losses will be great.

Only a few will be ready when I come for them. Why is this so? It is because only a few desire to press into ME. The world is so tantalizing and the people cannot take their hands off of her. Break free and follow hard after ME, your GOD and ONLY HOPE.

Only by giving ME a FULL SURRENDER with HUMBLE SUBMISSION, REPENTANCE OF SIN, and a DESIRE FOR A FULL OIL LAMP leading to intimacy with ME, your GOD, will you find the salvation for your soul.

The world will soon never be the same again. It is about to face horror and destruction: the like has never been seen before. It will only be MY Grace and Mercy that will finally put an end to it all and only by MY Power will the evil be stopped. Men cannot stop what is coming and they will not be able to keep it at bay. Fear and destruction and terror will reign supreme over the earth during the greatest tribulation man has ever seen.

Come out with ME when I call up MY few, MY bride, MY select. Only a few are going—very few. These ones know ME in the secret place where very few are willing to tread. Only a few want to make time to really know their GOD. This is what I require: intimacy. MY Word is very clear about this matter. Come now and get to know ME in the intimate place. There is no replacement for this closeness. The world cannot compare to eternity spent with GOD.

Children, your time is running out. MY enemy is getting closer and closer to his goal of tyranny over the people. I cannot wait forever on the hearts of MY people. Most are too far gone to recover. You need to turn and face your GOD before the time is too late.

These Words are True. Consider them seriously.

This is your GOD.

Your BRIDEGROOM Cometh.

Matthew 6:24: No man can serve two masters: for either he will hate the one, and love the other; or else he will hold to the one, and despise the other. Ye cannot serve GOD and mammon.

Luke 17:26-30: ^{26}And as it was in the days of Noah, so shall it be also in the days of the SON of man. ^{27} They did eat, they drank, they married wives, they were given in marriage, until the day that Noah entered into the ark, and the flood came, and destroyed them all. ^{28}Likewise also as it was in the days of Lot; they did eat, they drank, they bought, they sold, they planted, they builded; ^{29}But the same day that Lot went out of Sodom it rained fire and brimstone from heaven, and destroyed them all. ^{30} Even thus shall it be in the day when the SON of man is revealed.

Revelation 7:9-14: ^{9}After this I beheld, and, lo, a great multitude, which no man could number, of all nations, and kindreds, and people, and tongues, stood before the throne, and before the LAMB, clothed with white robes, and palms in their hands; ^{10}And cried with a loud voice, saying, Salvation to our GOD which sitteth upon the throne, and unto the LAMB. ^{11}And all the angels stood round about the throne, and about the elders and the four beasts, and fell before the throne on their faces, and worshipped GOD, ^{12}Saying, Amen: Blessing, and glory, and wisdom, and thanksgiving, and honour, and power, and might, be unto our GOD forever and ever. Amen. ^{13}And one of the elders answered, saying unto me, What are these which are arrayed in white robes? And whence came they? ^{14}And I said unto him, Sir, thou knowest. And he said to me, These are they which came out of great tribulation, and have washed their robes, and made them white in the blood of the LAMB.

Matthew 25:1-10: Then shall the kingdom of heaven be likened unto ten virgins, which took their lamps, and went forth to meet the bridegroom. ^{2}And five of them were wise, and five were foolish.

³They that were foolish took their lamps, and took no oil with them: ⁴But the wise took oil in their vessels with their lamps. ⁵While the bridegroom tarried, they all slumbered and slept. ⁶And at midnight there was a cry made, Behold, the bridegroom cometh; go ye out to meet him. ⁷Then all those virgins arose, and trimmed their lamps. ⁸And the foolish said unto the wise, Give us of your oil; for our lamps are gone out. ⁹But the wise answered, saying, Not so; lest there be not enough for us and you: but go ye rather to them that sell, and buy for yourselves. ¹⁰And while they went to buy, the bridegroom came; and they that were ready went in with him to the marriage: and the door was shut.

Psalm 91: He that dwelleth in the secret place of the MOST HIGH shall abide under the shadow of the ALMIGHTY.

Release Your Devotion To The World

Words of the LORD:

"Don't be blinded by your lack of knowledge and resistance to Truth—MY Truth."

(Words Received from Our LORD by Susan, November 14, 2012)

Let US begin:

Children, it is I, your LORD:

There is a lesson I am about to teach the world. I am about to show MYSELF strong. I am about to unleash MY wrath. I am about to allow the people to know their GOD in a way they have not known ME before. I will allow these people to see ME as a GREAT SAVIOR of MY ardent followers and then the GREAT JUDGE over the evil and wicked who reject ME wholesale.

This earth is an abomination to ME—a stench and a stink under MY Holy Nose. The protection over this land I have provided is slipping free. I am releasing MY Grip over the earth making ready to turn it over to MY adversary who is waiting in the wings to carry out his treachery and destruction. You have not known this much evil coming over the world at once.

MY children, you have become accustom to MY Hand of protection. You have not really seen what can happen when your GREAT GOD releases HIS Grip and turns the world over to evil leadership. You have not experienced the world without your GOD's Protection in place.

This world will soon not look the same as MY opponent and evil men take over and the light of MY bride is removed from your presence. She is bright with MY HOLY SPIRIT WHO restrains the evil from reigning in full force. Soon this restraint will be removed and the antichrist will rise up to destroy those who are left behind who turn back to ME for their salvation. HE will not allow anyone who claims ME as their SAVIOR and GOD to run free or to live in peace. All will know the penalty of being loyal to ME.

This tyranny is forming now. Don't be blinded by your lack of knowledge and resistance to Truth - MY Truth. Come to your senses. READ MY WORD. Awaken to the understanding of the hour you live in and make things right with your GOD. SURRENDER to ME in a COMPLETE and FULL SURRENDER. REPENT to MY Holiness. FORGIVE those around you leaving no stone unturned. Come to ME and RECEIVE A FULL OIL LAMP.

Read and study MY Word and get to know your GOD in an intimate way by seeking ME in the secret place. Come to know your GOD. Release your devotion to the world. Make time for your GOD.

There is no other way. I AM THE ONLY WAY by which men can come to the FATHER. Only by believing and knowing ME. All other roads and paths lead to hell.

I am SURE FOOTING - SOLID GROUND - I am your PROTECTION in the storm. Come to ME now. Get to know ME now. I am holding your place at MY Table, MY Wedding Banquet. Only you have the power to choose for ME. Make your choice. I have made a way for you. The door will not stay open forever.

This is your LORD, SAVIOR, STRONG TOWER.

Joshua 23:15: Therefore it shall come to pass, that as all good things are come upon you, which the LORD your GOD promised you; so shall the LORD bring upon you all evil things, until HE have destroyed you from off this good land which the LORD your GOD hath given you.

Zechariah 14:6-7: And it shall come to pass in that day, that the light shall not be clear, nor dark: [7]But it shall be one day which shall be known to the LORD, not day, nor night: but it shall come to pass, that at evening time it shall be light.

2 Thessalonians 2:7: For the mystery of iniquity doth already work: only HE WHO now letteth will let, until HE be taken out of the way.

Hosea 4:6: MY people are destroyed for lack of knowledge: because thou hast rejected knowledge, I will also reject thee, that thou shalt be no priest to ME: seeing thou hast forgotten the law of thy GOD, I will also forget thy children.

Matthew 25:10: And while they went to buy, the bridegroom came; and they that were ready went in with him to the marriage: and the door was shut.

Sun, 25 Nov 2012

Subject: The LORD's Words: "Your half-hearted pursuit of ME will never gain you a place at MY Marriage Table."

The LORD's Words for Today (Posted at www.End-Times-Prophecy.Com)

SOON AND VERY SOON

JESUS CHRIST will come to take HIS blood bought, surrendered bride to her heavenly home. ARE YOU SURE YOU ARE READY?

DON'T IGNORE THE SIGNS

Blatant worldwide evil, unashamed wickedness, rampant chaos in all levels of society, and

MOST OF ALL A HATRED OF THE TRUE GOD OF THE BIBLE, TRASHING HIS CHARACTER AND COMMANDS, HAS RAPIDLY INCREASED OVER THE LAST FEW YEARS.

Extreme weather, a myriad of earthquakes as never before; Israel surrounded by those who would annihilate every Jew and Christian on this planet.

GOD's Word is no longer the foundation of the United States. The fourth president James Madison, known as the Father of our Constitution, declared, "We've staked our future on our ability to follow the Ten Commandments with all of our heart." NO MORE! It is illegal to have a copy displayed in our public schools.

"Now when these things begin to happen, look up and lift up your heads, because your redemption draws near." Luke 21:28

JESUS IS APPEARING IN VISIONS AND DREAMS ALL OVER THIS PLANET

JEWS: I can personally testify to that. A Jewish lady, whom I knew at work, came to me and desired something serious. She told me that YESHUA came to her in a dream, put HIS Hand on her shoulder and said, "I am your FRIEND!" She came from a strict background. We went to lunch and I gave her a Jewish Bible and had her to read Isaiah 53. When she was finished she looked at me with tears in her eyes and knew exactly who Isaiah was talking about – YESHUA !

http://www.scribd.com/doc/42277052/Rabbi-Reveals-Name-of-the-Messiah "A few months before he died, one of the nation's most prominent rabbis, Yitzhak Kaduri, supposedly wrote the name of the MESSIAH on a small note which he requested would remain sealed until now. When the note was unsealed, it revealed what many have known for centuries: YEHOSHUA, or YESHUA (JESUS), is the MESSIAH...His son Rabbi David Kaduri confirmed, however, that in his last year, his father had talked and dreamed almost exclusively about the MESSIAH and his coming. "My father has met the MESSIAH in a vision," he said, "and told us that he would come soon."...But there they were, scribbled in the rabbi's own hand. When we asked what those symbols meant, Rabbi David Kaduri said they were "signs of the angel." Pressed further about the meaning of the "signs of the angel," he said he had no idea. Rabbi David Kaduri went on to explain that only his father had had a spiritual relationship with GOD and had met the MESSIAH in his dreams."

JESUS OUR BRIDEGROOM IS WARNING HIS BRIDE TO REPENT

CHRISTIANS: Joel 2:28 "And it shall come to pass afterward That I will pour out MY SPIRIT on all flesh; Your sons and your daughters shall prophesy, Your old men shall dream dreams, Your young men shall see visions.

JESUS is showing up to young and old alike telling them to warn HIS bride that HE is coming very soon and they need to be right with HIM. Here is an example from this link: http://end-times-prophecy.com/blog/

Update on Dreams/Visions: A dear friend from Switzerland who sees the LORD in visions wrote this note about two weeks ago: She wrote: Friday night, I was at a prayer meeting, there was a pastor from England who preached. During the worship time, I saw in a vision YAHUSHUA, HE told me: "Daughter, I'm coming." Then after that, the preacher looked at me and said that the LORD talks to people and tells them things. Since August, twice she has seen a vision of CHRIST coming down through the clouds and twice she has heard the sound of a trumpet blowing very loudly.

Then she wrote me again this note about a week ago: Hi Susan! Greetings in the name of YAHUSHUA. As I told you, yesterday at about 6:20 pm, I felt lifted up, I couldn't feel my steps, I felt so light. I thought it was the rapture, it was so real and this sensation of going up was amazing. I saw loads of blue lights around me and I knew there were angels around me. So I told ABBA FATHER : "Is it the rapture?" I repented and told HIM that I don't want to be left behind. I've experienced being lifted up last week too, but yesterday it was stronger with those blue lights around me.

Also a good friend's husband had a three-part vision a couple weeks ago : He saw first a bright white cross. Then next, he saw people going up into the air—he said there were "hundreds" not thousands that he saw and finally, he saw himself floating among very bright stars and he said it was a very peaceful sensation.

Finally, I want to add that yet another friend has reported finding white feathers all over her home that are showing up just recently.

Words of the LORD:

"Your half-hearted pursuit of ME will never gain you a place at MY Marriage Table."

(Words Received from Our LORD by Susan, November 20, 2012)

I am ready to give you a new Word. This Word is for MY people.

Children of GOD:

You are before MY Face. I see MY church: those who worship ME in Love and Truth; those who seek ME through MY Word and who pursue ME through Truth. MY children who truly love their GOD seek ME relentlessly through faith, believing I am REAL. They want ALL of ME ALL the time. They make time for ME throughout their days.

These children know their GOD because they have taken time to pursue ME in their hearts. They don't reject ME for the world. They find ME worthy of their time. I fill their days because they enjoy MY Company. They reject the ways and things of the world that pull them away from ME and MY Truth. Their time is MY Time. They have given themselves over to ME. They are no longer their own and MY enemy's.

Their heart is devoted to ME, MY Will, MY Ways, and the things I pursue. MY Pursuit is their pursuit. They are MY Hands and MY

Feet. Their selfless giving replenishes many. This is MY Way, the Way MY church embraces—MY bride, MY light.

Soon I will take these out from the earth—those who light the way in darkness—a dark, evil earth. I will remove the last remaining light on earth—MY SPIRIT WHO shines through MY bride and MY church WHO bears the LIGHT of MY HOLY SPIRIT. All will be removed and that which restrains evil will be taken out of the way. Evil will then take over in full force.

I will take you to safety when I come for MY bride. You must come to ME with a full surrender, repentance with a humbled heart, forgiveness from a repentant heart to those around you. You must seek a full oil lamp and the filling of MY HOLY SPIRIT. You must read MY Word. Get acquainted with ME by coming to ME in the secret place where we can meet and know each other.

I am not elusive or hard to find. I am always near. I am always ready to meet you wherever you are but you must humble yourself, surrender your all, and desire to have ME in all MY Fullness. I will not entertain a half-hearted relationship—one in which you long for the things of this world as much as GOD. This can never be. Either you want all of ME or none at all.

I do not take lightly to those who pursue mammon and the lusts of the flesh and the things of this world—and yet still believe that I, GOD can be consigned to a small portion of your life. This is evil and when we meet fact-to-face I will spit you out.

Come to terms with what I require from you to be part of MY Kingdom and saved from the coming tribulation: punishment reserved for evil men. The hour is closing in and you must wash your robe in MY Blood if you wish to be found worthy of MY Coming rescue for MY bride.

Your half-hearted pursuit of ME will never gain you a place at MY Marriage Table. Think this through carefully. Your eternal salvation hinges on it. I will not leave those behind who love ME with passionate hearts and pursue ME through Truth from a filling of MY HOLY SPIRIT. This is what I require. Are you willing to pay the price to be with ME for eternity?

Very few have decided to lay their lives down, let go of the world, and very few are coming with ME. MY Scripture speaks it. See for yourself.

The hour approaches for MY Return. I am looking for those whose garments are ready.

This is THE BRIDEGROOM.

ROYAL DIADEM.

Mark 12:30: And thou shalt love the LORD thy GOD with all thy heart, and with all thy soul, and with all thy mind, and with all thy strength: this is the first commandment.

Numbers 15:39: And it shall be unto you for a fringe, that ye may look upon it, and remember all the commandments of the LORD, and do them; and that ye seek not after your own heart and your own eyes, after which ye use to go a whoring:

Luke 16:13: No servant can serve two masters: for either he will hate the one, and love the other; or else he will hold to the one, and despise the other. Ye cannot serve GOD and mammon.

2 Thessalonians 2:6-8: [6] And now ye know what withholdeth that he might be revealed in his time. [7] For the mystery of iniquity doth already work: only HE WHO now letteth will let, until he be taken out of the way. [8] And then shall that Wicked be revealed, whom the LORD shall consume with the SPIRIT of HIS Mouth, and shall destroy with the brightness of HIS Coming:

Revelation 3:16: So then because thou art lukewarm, and neither cold nor hot, I will spue thee out of MY Mouth.

1 Peter 4:18: And if the righteous scarcely be saved, where shall the ungodly and the sinner appear?

2 Peter 2:20-21: [20] For if after they have escaped the pollutions of the world through the knowledge of the LORD and SAVIOUR JESUS CHRIST, they are again entangled therein, and overcome, the latter end is worse with them than the beginning. [21] For it had been better for them not to have known the way of righteousness, than, after they have known it, to turn from the holy commandment delivered unto them.

There Is Very Little Time Left

Words of the LORD:

"MY Salvation never weakens—no one can replace it, or take from it, or add to it."

(Words Received from Our LORD by Susan, November 21, 2012)

Daughter, here is the Word:

Children, you need to listen to ME, your GOD. There is very little time left as MY enemy is consuming the land. He is taking over the earthen vessels—MY people. He is ruling over those who allow him into their hearts. He is taking over their beings and stealing their souls away with his lies and deception. He has captivated the people so that they refuse to listen to their True GOD: CREATOR of all mankind.

A man's soul is corrupted by evil until I place MY Hand upon him and he is drawn back to his CREATOR. When you feel the pull or draw of MY SPIRIT, HE is calling you back to ME—your LORD.

I laid MY Life down for you. I gave ALL: MY Sacrifice was complete—nothing was left undone. I became a Humble SERVANT of GOD to serve and meet the needs of the people, to show MYSELF Faithful, to give MY All to MY followers—those who would receive MY Message, MY Salvation: all who believe I am their GOD. This was MY Desire, to reach all men who would come to ME and receive MY Salvation for ALL time.

This Salvation is not diminished by time. It is just as potent now as the day I died on the cross for all men. MY Salvation never weakens—no one can replace it, or take from it, or add to it. MY Blood spilt is as powerful now as it ever will be. Take this gift, it is offered to you freely. It is available now—soon there will be a price to pay after MY church is removed. Those left behind will be required to lay down their lives to receive their salvation as MY enemy will require those who refuse his mark to taste death in exchange for refusing his control over them.

Choose for ME now and avoid this evil and tribulation. MY Salvation is free and available now. Come into MY Saving Grace and Mercy. Exchange your life of sin, and following MY enemy against MY Will, for the salvation of your soul. Receive MY SPIRIT in all HIS Fullness. Receive the gifts of MY SPIRIT as HE freely gives. Be clothed with the fruits of MY SPIRIT and receive a clean heart and a renewed mind. Now is the time to receive power through the indwelling of MY SPIRIT. This is MINE to give—yours for the asking.

Only you can choose. No one can choose this for you. Even I cannot force this gift on you. You must decide. Are you coming with ME or will I have to leave you behind? I want to spend eternity with you in MY Beautiful Heavens. Please choose for ME.

I am the LOVE of your life.

CREATOR—MAKER—DESIGNER of ALL life.

HUMBLE GOD.

2 Corinthians 4:6-7: ⁶For GOD, WHO Commanded the light to shine out of darkness, hath shined in our hearts, to give the light of the knowledge of the glory of GOD in the Face of JESUS CHRIST. ⁷But we have this Treasure in earthen vessels, that the excellency of the power may be of GOD, and not of us.

John 6:44: No man can come to ME, except the FATHER which hath sent ME draw him: and I will raise him up at the last day.

Mark 14:65: And some began to spit on HIM, and to cover HIS Face, and to buffet HIM, and to say unto HIM, Prophesy: and the servants did strike HIM with the palms of their hands.

Hebrews 2:9: But we see JESUS, WHO was made a little lower than the angels for the suffering of death, crowned with glory and honour; that HE by the grace of GOD should taste death for every man.

Sun, 2 Dec 2012

The LORD's Words: "Choose for holiness and MY Ways through a FULL surrender."

The LORD's Words for Today (Posted at www.End-Times-Prophecy.Com)

Ministry people: you will have to answer to GOD for remaining silent and allowing innocent people to remain in the belief that everything is normal in the world and that there is no reason to be alarmed or to turn to the LORD to prepare for HIS Return.

James 3: My brethren, be not many masters, knowing that we shall receive the greater condemnation.

5. I Cannot Wait On MY Bride Forever

Words of the LORD:

"I am a GOD True to MY Word. MY Word is coming to pass."

(The following letter was given by the LORD to Susan at the request of a church in Africa that wanted a message from the LORD for their service, November 21, 2012)

Let US Begin:

I am here to speak to MY church.

There is an uproar of major proportions coming. It will be coming to the whole earth. I am speaking of the great tribulations. This world is winding down from the direction it has been moving in—all around you can see the world crumbling and coming apart. Truth is not wanted anymore. Those who want it are few and far between.

I am about to show MYSELF LARGER than life to those who are slumbering. They will be startled from their sleep. Soon you will know the fury of MY Wrath. I will use people, weather, circumstances to make MY Point. So don't be caught asleep when I come for MY alert bride. No one will escape MY Wrath if they are left behind. No one will withstand what is coming. MY Blessing removed—MY Protecting Hand removed—MY enemy's wrath poured out full force: this is what's coming.

Prepare to escape when I come for MY true church. Very few are coming. This is an elite group known for their selfless love and devotion to ME: FULLY SURRENDERED to their GOD—FULLY OBEDIENT—READY TO SERVE OUT OF A CHEERFUL HEART—

EAGER TO FOLLOW AND PURSUE THE LOST AS MY CAPABLE HANDS AND FEET.

Now is the hour for your redemption and to go after others—tomorrow may be too late. Don't put off your pursuit of GOD, salvation, and rapture-readiness. These all go hand-in-hand. Don't let the distractions of this life lead you astray. Face your GOD. Surrender to MY Holy Face, repent freely and frequently.

Very few will be rescued. Let this warning be heeded. I cannot wait on MY bride forever. She is beautiful and I am ready for MY Wedding Celebration. Come while "Coming to your GOD" is available. Don't miss MY Offer. Many will not make it. This is a True Word. I do not mean to frighten you—only to awake you.

MY Truth stands the test of time. I am a GOD True to MY Word. MY Word is coming to pass. Don't disregard what has already been written and even now is happening exactly as I said it would.

Come and receive MY Hand of Rescue. Regrets will be high to those who could have received MY Salvation but chose to ignore it for the ways of the world. Woe to those who love the world and reject their GOD.

I am coming. Are you ready?

This is your LORD.

KING of kings, LORD of lords.

Matthew 7:14: Because strait is the gate, and narrow is the way, which leadeth unto life, and few there be that find it.

1 Peter 4:18: And if the righteous scarcely be saved, where shall the ungodly and the sinner appear?

1 Corinthians 9:26-27: I therefore so run, not as uncertainly; so fight I, not as one that beateth the air: ^{27}But I keep under my body, and bring it into subjection: lest that by any means, when I have preached to others, I myself should be a castaway.

2 Peter 2:20-22: ^{20}For if after they have escaped the pollutions of the world through the knowledge of the LORD and SAVIOUR JESUS CHRIST, they are again entangled therein, and overcome, the latter end is worse with them than the beginning. ^{21}For it had been better for them not to have known the way of righteousness, than, after they have known it, to turn from the holy commandment delivered unto them. ^{22}But it is happened unto them according to the true proverb, The dog is turned to his own vomit again; and the sow that was washed to her wallowing in the mire.

Matthew 7:13: Enter ye in at the strait gate: for wide is the gate, and broad is the way, that leadeth to destruction, and many there be which go in thereat:

Psalm 2:12: Kiss the SON, lest he be angry, and ye perish from the way, when his wrath is kindled but a little. Blessed are all they that put their trust in him.

Matthew 18:8: Wherefore if thy hand or thy foot offend thee, cut them off, and cast them from thee: it is better for thee to enter into life halt or maimed, rather than having two hands or two feet to be cast into everlasting fire.

Philippians 2:12: Wherefore, my beloved, as ye have always obeyed, not as in my presence only, but now much more in my absence, work out your own salvation with fear and trembling.

Choose For Holiness And My Ways Through A Full Surrender

Words of the LORD:

"Choose for holiness and MY Ways through a FULL surrender."

(Words Received from Our LORD by Susan, November 25, 2012)

Let US begin:

The world is coming apart into pieces. Piece by piece she is crumbling. The world cannot be sustained by hearts of evil: hearts that reject GOD. ONLY I, GOD can turn this world around—only MY Love and All-Encompassing Power could turn this world back to the flawless world it once was.

MY Hand is being lifted away so that evil can have its way with a wicked, depraved people—people who believe GOD is not real and who want to rebel against MY Holy Standards for living in the world. Without GOD to answer to, men think they can do what they want apart from MY Guiding Hand. Soon, many will see that this is nothing but a great delusion fostered by their evil leader they are following into the pits of everlasting hell, death, and destruction: punishment for disobedience and rebellion.

I want to speak on the Holiness of your GOD—I am Holy and Pure. MY Holiness is life, everlasting life: the foundation of eternity with GOD. Your spirit cannot come into MY Pure Presence without the full endowment of MY HOLY SPIRIT indwelling your spirit to conform your spirit into MY Image thus making you presentable to come into MY Eternal Presence.

To receive the fullness of MY SPIRIT, you must SURRENDER YOUR ALL to make room for MY SPIRIT. "Self" must be eliminated to make room for MY All-consuming Power and Will. Without MY Will in your life, you are not MINE, but operating in the will of MY enemy, leading you into corruption, rebellion against your HOLY GOD. Your spirit and soul are corrupting your flesh to do evil works against a Holy GOD, your CREATOR.

Your spirit can only be made perfect by being made into MY Perfect Image, then and only then, do you receive the salvation of your soul and then are you presentable to dwell with a HOLY GOD.

Repentance; the surrender of your life and of a humbled heart—this is what I require to release MY SPIRIT into your spirit in complete fullness—a full oil lamp lighting your way to freedom to walk securely with your GOD.

I am coming to remove MY bride: those whose spirits are in MY Perfect Image. Anything else is a partial and incomplete surrender, lukewarm offering, to which I will reject in favor of those who choose to give their ALL in exchange for the love of the world. Focus on the world in exchange for the salvation of your soul—this is the evil trade off people are exchanging for their GOD to make love to evil. I have given all to rescue MY children, yet they settle for less—a dance with wickedness exchanging beauty and life everlasting.

Choose for holiness and MY Ways through a FULL surrender. Time is dwindling. The world spirals downward into darkness—a world apart from its GOD. Come apart—be set apart from all that is evil. Be part of the very few who want true salvation. Few will come out to safety. I will bring you into MY World of everlasting peace, but you must desire it. Choose for it. The choice is yours to make.

Choose Holiness,

I AM HOLY - YOU BE HOLY.

Psalm 29:2: Give unto the LORD the glory due unto HIS Name; worship the LORD in the beauty of holiness.

Leviticus 11:45: For I am the LORD that bringeth you up out of the land of Egypt, to be your GOD: ye shall therefore be holy, for I am holy.

Ephesians 4:24: And that ye put on the new man, which after GOD is created in righteousness and true holiness.

Hebrews 12:14: Follow peace with all men, and holiness, without which no man shall see the LORD:

Colossians 3:10: And have put on the new man, which is renewed in knowledge after the image of HIM that created him:

Psalm 4:3: But know that the LORD hath set apart him that is godly for HIMSELF: the LORD will hear when I call unto HIM.

1 Peter 1:16: Because it is written, Be ye holy; for I am Holy.

Mark of the Beast: An Overview

Revelation 20:4: And I saw thrones, and they sat upon them, and judgment was given unto them: and I saw the souls of them that were beheaded for the witness of JESUS, and for the word of GOD, and which had not worshipped the beast, neither his image, neither had received his mark upon their foreheads, or in their hands; and they lived and reigned with CHRIST a thousand years.

Everything now is being bar coded. The Mark of the Beast is the RFID chip which is now in the form of both chip and mark and is the tracking device that coordinates with the comprehensive, universal bar coding everywhere. It will be inserted in the hand and forehead based on an expensive study done by the industry as to where to best place the chip in a human.

Revelation 13:16: And he causeth (cause is defined as to be the cause of; bring about; precipitate; be the reason for) all, both small and great, rich and poor, free and bond, to receive a mark in their right hand, or in their foreheads: The first formal documentation legalized to included human micro-chipping as described in the bible is in the United States Healthcare Bill that just passed.

Why Human Micro-chipping?

James 4:4: Ye adulterers and adulteresses, know ye not that the friendship of the world is enmity with GOD? Whosoever therefore will be a friend of the world is the enemy of GOD.

Micro-chipping will lead to knowledge and access to information about everyone who receives it by the immoral antichrist leaders controlling it. There are two choices for people to make: satan and the world's way OR GOD's Way. GOD is omnipotent, omniscient, and omnipresent. Satan always wants to copy GOD and this system is an attempt to have the same all-knowing control as GOD—but beware those who buy into this man-made system versus GOD's Kingdom. You can either choose the beast's mark in your forehead or GOD's Mark as you can see in these scriptures:

Revelation 14:9-10: [9] And the third angel followed them, saying with a loud voice, If any man worship the beast and his image, and receive his mark in his forehead, or in his hand, [10] The same shall drink of the wine of the wrath of GOD, which is poured out without mixture into the cup of HIS indignation; and he shall be tormented with fire and brimstone in the presence of the holy angels, and in the presence of the LAMB:

Revelation 22:4: And they shall see HIS Face; and HIS Name shall be in their foreheads.

Revelation 14:1: And I looked, and, lo, a LAMB stood on the mount Sion, and with HIM an hundred forty and four thousand, having HIS FATHER's Name written in their foreheads.

World's Growing Acceptance of Microchip Technology

Where does the culture stand in acceptance of the microchip technology today? This world is very close to accepting the reality of a chip inserted in the body. Already thousands, perhaps as many as two million people, industry experts believe, have been voluntarily micro-chipped. Here is some insight on the progress the world is making in moving toward micro-chipping:

The primary promoters of this technology, banking and credit card companies, are moving us to what they proudly promote as a "cashless society." Mastercard has information on the future of cashless payments found at this link: http://newsroom.mastercard.com/future-of-payments-stream/

Right now the thrust on everyone, what you could say, is just one step away from human micro-chipping. The next closest thing to the microchip in the body is the handling and adjustment to the microchip outside the body with Mastercard's program PayPass™ contactless, cashless payment system also called Tap & Go™ with an embedded microchip and antenna as seen at these links: http://www.mastercard.us/paypass.html#/home/ and http://newsroom.mastercard.com/2011/04/16/bringing-tap-and-go-to-the-masses-and-my-brother/ This link shows how a recent event utilized the microchip in a wristband also demonstrating the next closest thing to human micro-chipping: Isle of Wight Festival Goers to Receive First-Ever Auto Top-up MasterCard® PayPass™ Wristband: http://newsroom.mastercard.com/?s=rfid

Looking Back to See Ahead

To know the future sometimes you need to see the past. Human tracking and marking was already implemented during the Nazi reign over Germany with the aid of computer giant IBM. Jews and others in Nazi concentration camps were tracked with tattoos and through IBM's custom punch-card system. Today, IBM says they do not have historical records on this program. But historians who studied the program say it was IBM working with Hitler for profit. Here are details on that program: Globalist Controlled IBM Assisted Hitler in Organizing Concentration Camps--The Tattoo Used in Auschwitz Was Originally An IBM Code Number:

http://decryptedmatrix.com/live/globalist-controlled-ibm-assisted-hitler-in-organizing-concentration-camps/

and also this article on probing IBM's Nazi connection: Since its publication in February, Edwin Black's book "IBM and the Holocaust: The Strategic Alliance Between Nazi Germany and America's Most Powerful Corporation" has stirred unprecedented controversy among students of the Holocaust, American enterprise, and information technology: http://news.cnet.com/2009-1082-

269157.html The difference between what will happen in the not so distant future according to the Bible is the same as Nazi Germany only it's the same scenario "on global high-tech steroids."

Right now these government agencies are looking to use these new technologies on people soon: the military:

http://www.mobiledia.com/news/134354.htm

and the Food Stamps Program:

http://www.pakalertpress.com/2012/11/26/use-of-rfid-tracking-technology-to-be-mandatory-in-us-food-stamp-program-2/?utm_source=feedburner&utm_medium=feed&utm_campaign=Feed%3A+pakalert+%28Pak+Alert+Press%29&utm_content=Google+Feedfetcher

Don't watch dates for these proposed human chipping programs as a key to the timing of the rapture event (as if you can base your watching for the LORD's Return on man's timetables)—the rapture event timing, only known by GOD, will in fact trigger the use of the micro-chipping according to the Bible. The rapture is indeed at the door and ministry people and Christians need to be vigilant in telling others and stop embracing the world that is an enmity to their SAVIOR.

Mon, 10 Dec 2012

The LORD's Words: "The light will be snuffed out after I remove MY pre cious oil-filled lamps."

The LORD's Words for Today (Posted at www.End-Times-Prophecy.Com)

Dear Faithful Followers of CHRIST:

This is a hard piece to write—but I inquired the LORD in it and HE said, "Write it—the people are going to die if you don't tell them the Truth." Well that is good enough for me.

A couple summers ago, I went to a mainstream denomination church camp meeting as a visitor. I was sitting in the dining commons while about 100 or so people were gathered eating, laughing, talking.... I was on my computer at the time because of the wifi connection there and the LORD spoke to me and I was stunned—shocked about what HE said: "THEY ARE ALL LOST—THEY TALK TO EACH OTHER BUT THEY DON'T TALK TO ME."

I am here to tell you that WHOLE CONGREGATIONS ARE GOING TO BE LEFT BEHIND AT THE TIME OF THE RAPTURE.

WHY?

Revelation 3:16: So then because thou art lukewarm, and neither cold nor hot, I will spue thee out of MY Mouth.

The reason is the people are not getting the TRUTH at their mainstream churches. Because of GOD's great grace and mercy people have decided to disregard the LORD's commandments and believe they are obsolete for this time. But GOD did not dump the commandments because of the saving grace and mercy of CHRIST's amazing sacrifice on the cross. How do we know? The New Testament says so:

Matthew 5:19: Whosoever therefore shall break one of these least commandments, and shall teach men so, he shall be called the least in the kingdom of heaven: but whosoever shall do and teach them, the same shall be called great in the kingdom of heaven.

John 14:15: If ye love ME, keep MY commandments.

1 John 3:22: And whatsoever we ask, we receive of HIM, because we keep HIS commandments, and do those things that are pleasing in HIS Sight.

1 John 5:2-3: 2By this we know that we love the children of GOD, when we love GOD, and keep his commandments. 3 For this is the love of GOD, that we keep HIS commandments: and HIS commandments are not grievous.

Revelation 14:12: Here is the patience of the saints: here are they that keep the Commandments of GOD, and the faith of JESUS.

Revelation 12:17: And the dragon was wroth with the woman, and went to make war with the remnant of her seed, which keep the commandments of GOD, and have the testimony of JESUS CHRIST.

Even though the commandments have not been outmoded as many believe; they are in effect and they are our guide for living. Yet even pastors flaunt the breaking of them to their congregation by calling for church services to be shortened so that the congregation can run out and shop and watch football games on the LORD's Holy Day. People are not called to repentance and remorse over spending their whole week watching secular media that blasphemes GOD in a million ways and participating in all forms of worldly anti-GOD pursuits. Mainstream churches today have created their own version of GOD to worship—a god of their own making—an idol—a god who doesn't require holiness and frequent repentance and remorse over sin committed before a Holy GOD.

The main denominational churches won't talk about end times and the obvious ways the world is turning its back to GOD toward overwhelming evil away from GOD pointing to the multiple signs GOD gave in the Bible signaling the coming of the LORD for HIS bride. This message is taboo in the mainstream churches—too radical—too hard for the mainstream church goers who love the world.

The mainline churches even believe that the ten commandments can't be kept and holiness can't be achieved so holiness isn't even promoted. They are partially right—they can't be kept in the flesh—but here is the key: by the AWESOME POWER OF THE HOLY SPIRIT given by the baptism of the HOLY SPIRIT by praying to receive it and by MAKING A FULL SURRENDER TO THE LORD and making HIM TOTAL LORD AND MASTER MOVING INTO GOD'S WILL—it is possible. GOD would never require something from people that is impossible. Luke 1:37: For with GOD nothing shall be impossible.

Matthew 3:11: I indeed baptize you with water unto repentance. But HE that cometh after me is mightier than I, WHOSE Shoes I am not worthy to bear: HE shall baptize you with the HOLY GHOST, and with fire:

The mainline churches fear the FIRE of the HOLY SPIRIT and the subsequent manifestations that follow which are always supernatural, if it is truly from the HOLY SPIRIT—such things as tongues (although not always such as the HOLY SPIRIT chooses HIMSELF to gift); prophecy (hearing the LORD's Voice); visions; healing gifts; spiritual discernment, and more. So many squirm at these HOLY SPIRIT Manifestations and want to boot the HOLY SPIRIT out of their churches—trouble with this is that CHRIST is ONE with the HOLY SPIRIT and the power of the HOLY SPIRIT is essential to do and be in GOD's WILL, a requirement to salvation and to perform the commandments of GOD that are still in effect and have not been rendered invalid even if men believe it so. (Read about the baptism of the HOLY SPIRIT in Acts 19).

And why do the mainline and so many of today's modern churches want to dispense with the HOLY SPIRIT in HIS completeness through the baptism of the HOLY SPIRIT? Because the Religious

Spirit—a demonic spirit—runs rampant and thrives in today's churches (trouble is the people can't see this without the Power of the HOLY SPIRIT that they are rejecting). It is the same religious spirit that makes people feel worse in their church experiences then outside of church in their daily living. It is the enemy within the church rejecting the move of the Power of the HOLY SPIRIT and creating discouragement for the church to move in the Will of GOD. Here is more information about the Religious Spirit: http://www.takehisheart.com/satanpythonreligious.htm

If You Choose Against Me…

Words of the LORD:

"Evil is gathering its forces together against mankind to destroy the children of men."

(Words Received from Our LORD by Susan, December 3, 2012)

I am ready to give you Words:

The hour approaches for MY Return. Soon the people will see they are being held captive by a cruel and harsh enemy. This enemy is so cruel and harsh, he wants to destroy and kill and pull MY children away from ME. I will not be able to keep MY children out of his hands if they persist in rejecting ME—their SAVIOR.

Only I can save you, but you must turn to ME. I cannot help you if you reject ME—you render ME useless in your life if you deny MY Existence. I must have control of your life through your FULL Surrender to ME before I can rescue you from the hand and wiles of MY enemy. HE is ruthless in his dealings with men. He knows how to lead men astray.

You are no match for him apart from ME, your LORD. I am the only ONE WHO has ALL POWER over him. I am the only ONE WHO can control him and render him useless in your life. Until you come to terms with this, you will be tormented by him in one form or another. He brings pain and suffering on all MY children in this fallen world. Only by MY Blood Covering received through a FULL surrender of your life over to ME can you be safe from the evil attacks he launches against you.

You must face ME. Repent of your lifetime of sin against your GOD and MAKER conducted under the control and leadership of MY enemy, who runs your life. Until you surrender your ALL into MY Hands and Safekeeping, you are not safe apart from ME as your LORD and MASTER. You are fair game of MY enemy and you will ultimately fall prey to his tricks and control over your life. Your destiny will be eternal hell, torture, and torment. This is by his design. He wants you to suffer in this life and the next. He rules you if you are not surrendered to ME. Although you believe you are your own ruler, you are under the control and leadership of an evil master apart from ME, your CREATOR.

Come to your senses—time is running out. Evil is gathering its forces together against mankind to destroy the children of men. Why do you waffle about this decision? Is the world so gratifying that you want to be apart from your MAKER for all eternity? This is your choice to make.

If you choose against ME, I will honor your choice and cast you away from MY Presence for ALL time to come. Your decision will then be final and eternal and there will be no turning back. Choose this day who you will serve—your enemy and MINE OR your CREATOR, GOD, and LOVER. You decide. Time is not on your side.

I am GOD ETERNAL.

John 10:10: The thief cometh not, but for to steal, and to kill, and to destroy: I am come that they might have life, and that they might have it more abundantly.

Matthew 10:28: And fear not them which kill the body, but are not able to kill the soul: but rather fear HIM which is able to destroy both soul and body in hell.

Matthew 12:31: Wherefore I say unto you, All manner of sin and blasphemy shall be forgiven unto men: but the blasphemy against the HOLY GHOST shall not be forgiven unto men.

Matthew 24:12: And because iniquity shall abound, the love of many shall wax cold.

Luke 10:17: And the seventy returned again with joy, saying, LORD, even the devils are subject unto us through THY Name.

Matthew 7:13: Enter ye in at the strait gate: for wide is the gate, and broad is the way, that leadeth to destruction, and many there be which go in thereat:

Words of the LORD:

"The light will be snuffed out after I remove MY precious oil-filled lamps."

(Words Received from Our LORD by Susan, December 5, 2012)

Yes, WE may begin:

Children, I am GOD ETERNAL—GLORIOUS SAVIOR. I came to save your souls. I come to lead you out—MY Coming was to glorify MY children to begin life abundant. I am a GOD WHO is willing to give of HIMSELF. I gave all—I am a LIVING GOD, a SAVING GOD, an ETERNAL FORCE…I am the LOVER of your soul.

Don't deny ME the pleasure of your company for eternity. I died so that I could be with you for eternity. I endured horrible treatment. I was laid low... I saw evil at its worst so that I could raise you to the best: MY Presence in eternity—MY Eternal Kingdom of everlasting beauty. This was MY Gift to mankind—a fallen race scarred by sin, beaten down by adversity.

MY creation, I have given life to, can choose its CREATOR or MY enemy to pursue. I came to earth in a great demonstration of love to reveal MY Heart as TEACHER, GUIDE, COMFORTER, HEALER, SAVIOR, and LOVER to MY lost, fallen creation. I came to demonstrate MY Great Love—there is NO greater love that can be expressed than GOD ETERNAL coming into humanity to be punished for the sins of MY creation.

You can accept this gift and be saved from eternal punishment—a life separated from GOD forever. You must choose to come into this gift. I give it freely, but time is running out for you to be rescued from the wrath to come.

MY wrath will be poured over this evil world for all its rebellion against ME and MY Ways. There will be a price to pay for rejection of GOD and the payment will be met by those who reject ME. You can avoid this strife and terror but you must submit your ALL to ME, holding nothing back, in exchange for MY Salvation and MY transformation to freedom.

I am ready to depart soon. All is growing evil against ME. Stay and face the worst if you choose or come out to safety with MY true followers. I give you this freedom to choose. I will not take anyone by force. MY enemy will take you by force if you stay. You will either be forced into his evil plans or die rejecting them. Either way will lead to death—death to salvation or death to destruction.

It will not be an easy time for MY tribulation saints—those who die for their faith. Choose life now and avoid this pain. I will take you with ME and take you up to eternal beauty. There are only moments before this world embraces evil and becomes completely dark. The light will be snuffed out after I remove MY precious oil-filled lamps. You will then see darkness like never before.

I cry out to you. Come away. Come apart from evil. Run to MY waiting arms. You decide: for or against ME. I can only take you now if you reject the world and all it stands for. These are the conditions you must meet. Few will meet them…few are going.

The offer is still available just like it was to the lost generation of Noah's time. I am a fair GOD. You are being warned. Let these Words stand the test of time…

Your GOD: PATIENT, KIND, LONGSUFFERING.

Jeremiah 30:19: And out of them shall proceed thanksgiving and the voice of them that make merry: and I will multiply them, and they shall not be few; I will also glorify them, and they shall not be small.

John 3:2: The same came to JESUS by night, and said unto HIM, RABBI, we know that THOU art a TEACHER come from GOD: for no man can do these miracles that THOU doest, except GOD be with HIM.

Acts 10:38: How GOD anointed JESUS of Nazareth with the HOLY GHOST and with power: WHO went about doing good, and healing all that were oppressed of the devil; for GOD was with HIM.

2 Samuel 22:3: The GOD of my ROCK; in HIM will I trust: HE is my SHIELD, and the HORN of my salvation, my HIGH TOWER, and my REFUGE, my SAVIOR; THOU savest me from violence.

6. Outside Of My Will, All Men Practice Evil

The LORD's Words: "Outside of MY Will, all men practice evil."

The LORD's Words for Today (Posted at www.End-Times-Prophecy.Com)

Words of the LORD:

"This is the end to which I lead MY church to begin: Everlasting Beauty with its Great and Glory-Filled GOD."

(Words Received from Our LORD by Susan, December 12, 2012)

Put these Words on paper daughter:

Children it is I, your LORD:

I am coming herewith. There will be a day coming that I will stand before you at MY Marriage Supper Table as your KING and BRIDEGROOM. We will raise our glasses and partake in each other's Love: MY true church—MY loyal bride.

I behold you bride: loyal in all your ways...Truthful...full of Light...lovers of righteousness...faithful to your LORD...purveyors of Truth leading others into the Light. This is MY church, MY followers: willing to lay down their lives before ME, grant ME control over their lives...moving in MY Will to do MY work to assist ME in building MY Kingdom: to help set the captives free, to hold back the enemy, to write the law upon MY children's hearts to follow through love and devotion by the Power of MY HOLY SPIRIT WHO controls their every move...walking in paths of righteousness toward the Great Prize before them: Eternal Salvation in the Glory of their FATHER to the end of Glory upon Glory, to bask in the Light of MY Everlasting Love.

This is the end to which I lead MY church to begin: Everlasting Beauty with its Great and Glory-Filled GOD—KING of the Universe, EVERLASTING POWER. I am GREATNESS UNSPEAKABLE, RICHES UNTOLD, TREASURES LAID UP FOR EVER. This awaits MY church who puts ME above all else in this life—a brief segment in time.

Come and enjoy an eternity of abundance with joy and delight in your EVERLASTING KING. This world is only a brief dance. Come dance with your GOD. Put down your cares—leave wickedness behind. Stop spoiling your frocks, quit handling evil. Come learn of Peace, Salvation, Holiness, and the Delights of Purity. Come rule and reign with ME in the great tomorrow ever after. I will raise you up to great heights in MY Eternal Kingdom if you will SURRENDER TO ME NOW.

Lay down your life before ME. Submit to ME YOUR ALL. I will put you on a High Place in MY Coming Kingdom where Peace, Love, Laughter rains down like a storm—a fever pitch storm of Everlasting Beauty.

This life pales by comparison to MY Coming Kingdom of Everlasting Delights and Pleasures at MY Right Hand. Dispense with your evil desires that you do willfully for the evil captain of your soul—MY adversary. His rule and reign is almost over. Don't bend your knee to this losing captain of terror. His kingdom will soon be destroyed and you with it if you carry on under his leadership.

Come over to MY Everlasting Power and Control—I will free you from his empowerment, to do evil over your life. I will wrap you in MY Arms of Love, place a crown on your head and a robe of purity over your shoulders. You will stand on SOLID GROUND—the ROCK—I am that ROCK.

Drop your resistance and follow ME. MY time to plead with you is running out.

This is your LORD...SAVIOR...MASTER of Your Soul.

Come whosoever will...

John 8:12: Then spake JESUS again unto them, saying, I am the LIGHT of the world: he that followeth ME shall not walk in darkness, but shall have the LIGHT of life.

Luke 4:18: The SPIRIT of the LORD is upon ME, because HE hath anointed ME to preach the gospel to the poor; HE hath sent ME to heal the brokenhearted, to preach deliverance to the captives, and recovering of sight to the blind, to set at liberty them that are bruised,

Hebrews 8:10: For this is the covenant that I will make with the house of Israel after those days, saith the LORD; I will put MY laws into their mind, and write them in their hearts: and I will be to them a GOD, and they shall be to ME a people:

Psalm 16:11: THOU wilt shew me the path of life: in THY Presence is fulness of joy; at THY Right Hand there are pleasures for evermore.

Psalm 95:1: O come, let us sing unto the LORD: let us make a joyful noise to the ROCK of our salvation.

Revelation 16:15: Behold, I come as a THIEF. Blessed is he that watcheth, and keepeth his garments, lest he walk naked, and they see his shame.

7. People Believe My Warnings And My Words Are A Joke

(Words Received from Our LORD by Susan, December 10, 2012)

Yes daughter, I am ready to proceed:

I am sending forth many Words: many dire warnings of the hardship ahead for those who do not heed MY Words and follow in MY Will. Darkness looms over the earth. It is apparent to those who are watching. Many are asleep, still sleeping—vehemently denying the times they are living in—rejecting their GOD, living outside MY Will.

Although many believe themselves right with ME, they are not paying attention to the times and are rejecting warnings I am putting forth in abundance. The people believe MY Warnings and MY Words a joke: they read MY Words and are blind to Truth. They are not being led by MY SPIRIT, so they are not being fed Truth and cannot see what lies up ahead over the ridge—they believe they know based on their own futuristic thinking. Only I, GOD knows exactly what the future holds and it is a far cry from what mankind is planning for itself. Imagine men made in GOD's Image believing they can know the future apart from GOD and inquiring of ME. Soon they will wish they had pursued ME and not looked for Truth in their own wicked hearts...deceiving hearts.

The plans of men will soon blow away like sand and those who don't grab ahold of MY Truth will find a very different reality soon. I am not a GOD WHO can be mocked, ridiculed, and reduced to nothingness without retribution. I cannot allow rebellion to go unchecked. It must be found and dealt with. So many will learn their rebellion cannot be hidden and all will be out in the open for all to see.

I do not take lightly to sin. I cannot tolerate it apart from MY Blood Covering, forgiveness, and mercy granted to those who seek for it out of a sincere heart. There is no other way for a HOLY GOD to respond to such ongoing evil. Soon the world will see the punishment its due for blaspheming MY Holy Name, and MY Great Sacrifice for mankind, and the persons of the HOLY TRINITY, the Royal Diadem.

There must be a price paid for sins and rejection of the offer made by GOD to counter the punishment set forth by GOD for this sin: MY Blood-bought Sacrifice on a hard cross. This was the payment for men's sins, yet men reject the very thing freely available to save them from their sentencing for rampant sin performed before GOD, WHO is HOLY.

I provided the clear path to MY Kingdom out to safety. I will lead you to it by MY SPIRIT, through the direction in MY Book.

Children, you must listen to MY warnings. There are dark days coming. The world is turning its back to its GOD CREATOR. I am not known by the people—very few really know ME. Very few will be coming out with ME when I come to rescue MY true church—MY beloved.

There is only a small portion who really reject the world and all its trappings—the things of this life that lead the eye astray from GOD and serving ME with a pure heart. Only by a closeness to ME can your robes be purified and your heart cleaned out, prepared for MY Presence.

Chase after ME. Now is the time. Run toward ME even as the world is running away from ME. This is the direction to safety. You will not be safe in the hands of MY enemy who rules the hearts of wicked men. Outside of MY Will, all men practice evil, so to be in MY Will you must surrender your ALL. Your life must be crucified and dead to "self." Only then, will you find the salvation of your soul.

These Words are True—none Truer. Chase after Truth before it is blotted out by the evil workings of MY enemy and those who belong to him. Know the hour you live in and turn to your GOD. I am your only hope. Lay your life down and I will raise you up when I pull MY church out.

Your intellect can't save you...

Only the changing of your heart by MY SPIRIT and MY Blood

Matthew 7:21: Not everyone that saith unto me, LORD, LORD, shall enter into the kingdom of heaven; but he that doeth the will of MY FATHER which is in heaven.

Matthew 12:50: For whosoever shall do the will of MY FATHER which is in heaven, the same is MY brother, and sister, and mother.

James 4:13-14: 13Go to now, ye that say, Today or tomorrow we will go into such a city, and continue there a year, and buy and sell, and get gain: 14Whereas ye know not what shall be on the morrow. For what is your life? It is even a vapour, that appeareth for a little time, and then vanisheth away.

Matthew 7:14: Because strait is the gate, and narrow is the way, which leadeth unto life, and few there be that find it.

Romans 8:13: For if ye live after the flesh, ye shall die: but if ye through the SPIRIT do mortify the deeds of the body, ye shall live.

James 4:8: Draw nigh to GOD, and HE will draw nigh to you. Cleanse your hands, ye sinners; and purify your hearts, ye double minded.

Sat, 22 Dec 2012

The LORD's Words: "Soon, only darkness will cover the earth when MY li ghts eternal are taken away."

The LORD's Words for Today (Posted at www.End-Times-Prophecy.Com)

Dear Faithful Friends of CHRIST:

Matthew 7:21-23: 21Not everyone that saith unto me, LORD, LORD, shall enter into the kingdom of heaven; but he that doeth the Will of MY FATHER which is in heaven. 22Many will say to me in that day, LORD, LORD, have we not prophesied in thy name? And in THY Name have cast out devils? And in THY Name done many wonderful works? 23And then will I profess unto them, I never knew you: depart from ME, ye that work iniquity.

All the good in the world isn't good UNLESS it is within the Will of GOD. So no matter how wonderful the works, outside the Will of the FATHER so called "good works" or "wonderful works" are on the same par with evil works. There is so much going on in the world that looks like it is "good." The trouble is its classified as the "knowledge of good" from the tree of knowledge of good and evil:

Genesis 2:9: And out of the ground made the LORD GOD to grow every tree that is pleasant to the sight, and good for food; the tree of life also in the midst of the garden, and the tree of knowledge of good and evil.

Genesis 2:17: But of the tree of the knowledge of good and evil, thou shalt not eat of it: for in the day that thou eatest thereof thou shalt surely die.

Why is "good" in the world outside of the Will of GOD so bad?: because the world convinces itself that it can do "good" apart from the intervention of GOD and HIS Perfect Will. The world flexes its muscle in the pride of "self" apart from GOD and ultimately this proclamation of greatness will fall flat on its face. Let's not forget that satan comes also as an angel of light convincing people that the "good" they see produced by the antichrist world can somehow be positive when in reality what looks well and fine on the outside is really like white-washed tombs: lovely on the outside but totally out of the saving Perfect Will of GOD and full of dead man's bones.

2 Corinthians 11:14: And no marvel; for satan himself is transformed into an angel of light.

How can anyone do the Will of the FATHER so that good works are actually GOD's good works? Surrender your ALL to the LORD—everything—even future plans—swapping your own personal plans for GOD's divine plans for your life. Imagine allowing your CREATOR to apply HIS Perfect Plans to the life HE Created?

8. Anything Can Become An Idol

Words of the LORD:

"Come like a child..."

(Words Received from Our LORD by Susan, December 18, 2012)

Yes Susan, WE can begin. I will give you Words:

It is astounding the numbers of people who refuse to believe that I, GOD am real and that MY Coming is soon: this because, the people are tantalized by the world and the lure of the devil. He comes as an angel of light to attract and to allure the people away from their GOD—their CREATOR.

The people do not care to come to their senses. They only want to run and play in the streets of evil with their dark companions and enemy of their soul. He lurks at every corner enticing MY children away from Truth, feeding them lies. Disguising himself as what looks good and inviting. Anything can become an idol corrupting their soul, leading MY children to hell: anything that comes between US pulls you away from MY Word...forging an intimate relationship with ME...taking you from being in the center of MY Will for your life—the Kingdom work I have set for you to do. All this is destroyed, when you focus on everything but your GOD—at the design and destructive planning of MY adversary: cruel and cold-hearted. His desire is to take out as many of MY children as possible leading them into everlasting hell apart from their CREATOR GOD for eternity—a large price to pay for a little fling with sin in this brief stretch of time: your life on earth.

So few will come apart from the world and the evil dealings of MY enemy to prepare themselves for MY Coming. Many will be standing stunned after I arrive and remove MY ready children who are watching expectantly for their LORD and MASTER. Watchers are awake, lamps fully prepped fueled by the Power of MY SPIRIT—the Everlasting FLAME.

When I come to rescue the church out of the evil world only those purified by the Power of MY SPIRIT…made in MY Image…dead to 'self'…cleaned by MY Word… washed in MY Blood, only these will be recognized and plucked out to freedom and safety. All others, I will not recognize.

Come surrender your life. I extend MY Hand to you—walk with ME. Come, know and understand MY Ways. Embrace MY Words given through MY Book to the end of your Salvation, to the goal of your eternal bliss: realized by the keeping of your soul readied for the Day of Rapture—that is right at hand. Your fate will be sealed soon in hell if you don't follow ME.

The choice is simple: don't make it hard for yourself. Salvation made easy by MY Hard Work on a cross. What could be more simple? Even a child can grasp this Truth. Come like a child…

KEEPER of the children…

Matthew 18:3: And said, Verily I say unto you, Except ye be converted, and become as little children, ye shall not enter into the kingdom of heaven.

1 John 2:15: Love not the world, neither the things that are in the world. If any man love the world, the love of the FATHER is not in him.

1 Peter 5:8: Be sober, be vigilant; because your adversary the devil, as a roaring lion, walketh about, seeking whom he may devour:

Genesis 1:27: So GOD created man in HIS OWN IMAGE, in the IMAGE of GOD created HE him; male and female created HE them.

Ephesians 5:26: That HE might sanctify and cleanse it with the washing of water by the word,

Words of the LORD:

"Soon, only darkness will cover the earth when MY lights eternal are taken away."

(Words Received from Our LORD by Susan, December 20, 2012)

December 20, 2012

Precious children, it is I, your LORD addressing you:

The time has come to focus on GOD—your LORD and SAVIOR. There is nowhere else to turn—nowhere else to find answers. The world is deplete of Truth. It is full of lies and deceit. There is only sadness, death, and decay ahead for a world floundering apart from GOD.

There are dark days ahead. You are only seeing a hint of what's coming—a world run by evil: evil leaders, immoral men, demonic-inspired terror. That is what is ahead for those who refuse MY Truth and reject ME as their LORD and MASTER by running to MY enemy instead.

Tear yourself free from the control and leadership of evil—only under MY complete LORDSHIP and Control given ME by your FULL SURRENDER will you be released from this evil control. Only by submitting to ME FULLY through a strong desire in your heart to be set free from the grasp of the enemy can your soul and spirit belong to ME—given over to the salvation of your life pulled from an evil kingdom on earth and a future of unending torment, apart from GOD ALMIGHTY, in hell.

You must choose. Do you wish to be part of MY Eternal Kingdom or do you want to continue on your way down the broad road of destruction you have been running on since birth? Only you can decide to move off the wide pathway to hell and pull yourself free to the narrow way, to MY Kingdom Ever Lasting.

There is only ONE WAY to make it onto this single lane, narrow way to freedom, eternal beauty—delights in MY Heavenly Kingdom. Come before ME on bended knee with a heart of remorse and a sincere desire to have MY Eternal Leadership and Companionship. This is truly the choice before ALL men. Most disregard this choice, fall away, are distracted by the world and MY enemy. Most are deceived by traditions of men and lack of knowledge because of their rebellious hearts and desires to run apart from their GOD, CREATOR and MY Instruction through MY Word, MY Book.

Soon, I will pull away MY True church, also known as MY bride, to safety out of this evil world while the world turns to evil, terror, and destruction from MY punishment, while I allow the world to have its way: to run apart from MY Protecting Hand.

Choose to live with ME for eternity and the bounty of MY Love Ever Lasting or choose eternal damnation. Life is set before you. Reach for it. I can only set it in front of you. I cannot force you into MY Love.

For those who choose MY Love there will be no end to the joy they receive. This is MY Promise—does MY Word not speak it? Soon, only darkness will cover the earth when MY lights eternal are taken away—be among the eternal lights coming with their LORD.

This is the "FUTURE DELIGHT" Speaking.

Matthew 7:13: Enter ye in at the strait gate: for wide is the gate, and broad is the way, that leadeth to destruction, and many there be which go in thereat:

Hosea 4:6: MY people are destroyed for lack of knowledge: because thou hast rejected knowledge, I will also reject thee, that thou shalt be no priest to ME: seeing thou hast forgotten the law of thy GOD, I will also forget thy children.

Mark 7:8: For laying aside the commandment of GOD, ye hold the tradition of men, as the washing of pots and cups: and many other such like things ye do.

Deuteronomy 30:15: See, I have set before thee this day life and good, and death and evil;

Deuteronomy 30:19: I call heaven and earth to record this day against you, that I have set before you life and death, blessing and cursing: therefore choose life, that both thou and thy seed may live:

Philippians 2:15: That ye may be blameless and harmless, the sons of GOD, without rebuke, in the midst of a crooked and perverse nation, among whom ye shine as lights in the world;

Sun, 23 Dec 2012

The LORD's Words: A Special Message: "Tell the people I am coming soon , for many will perish."

The LORD's Words for Today (Posted at www.End-Times-Prophecy.Com)

Dear Faithful Friends of CHRIST:

My close friend, Donna, had a dream last night and we want to share it with you with a Letter received from the LORD about the dream:

DONNA WRITES: The LORD APPEARED TO ME IN A DREAM LAST NIGHT. I saw HIS Face clearly, HE was solemn and was wearing a kingly robe and a significant gold crown. HE was kneeling. HE said to me, "Tell the people I am coming soon, for many will perish." I immediately woke up and HE said to me: "Do not be afraid for I am with you always." It was 4:58 a.m.

The LORD wants us to move towards HIM quickly. We must diligently read our bibles and pray every day. Pray to have a full oil lamp and be rapture ready and in HIS Will. Pray to forgive all people of all things at all times. Repent of our sins daily, those known and unknown. Put down all secular interests and pursue HIM as your ONLY HOPE because HE IS OUR ONLY HOPE!

Donna called me and told me about her dream encounter the next day and after I hung up the phone the LORD spoke to me and said for me to get my journal and that HE wanted me to take down HIS Words regarding her dream encounter and to send this message out to everyone with her dream:

Words of the LORD:

"I am coming soon.

MY Return is now imminent."

9. I Am True To My Words

(Words Received from Our LORD by Susan, December 21, 2012)

Susan, listen to MY Words—I have Words and I want you to write them down:

Children, it is I, your LORD.

I am the ALMIGHTY GOD.

I am the TAKER and KEEPER of lights.

I have a great burden to share. MY Heart is broken. I am undone with sadness. I am overwhelmed to the point of great sorrow. You must listen as I speak:

I am coming soon. MY Return is now imminent. So few are paying attention. They do not want to believe that I, GOD am True to MY Words and that MY Words will come to pass.

There will be many lost in this coming hour. Many will reject MY Truth. Many are looking the other way back to the world. They want nothing with their GOD. They have chosen against ME. They are moving away from ME. I am distraught but cannot convince them otherwise though I cry out.

I speak through MY people, MY messengers, MY signs, MY Word. All the messages have gone out to warn the people. The people just refuse to believe ME. I have left nothing to chance. The warnings have been profuse. I have been abundantly gracious in MY Warnings. I have tried to warn all those who would listen. I have spoken through those of all ages, in all nations. There can be no one without excuse. All will be held accountable who have been disobedient and rejected MY Words of warning through the various means I have sent them.

Soon the world will see the reality of these Words—MY Heart aches in anguish over the children who will be lost for eternity. This sorrowful hour is soon approaching. This is a great junction in time in which MY Word Spoken will come about and the people will know that I, GOD am True to MY Word.

I am lingering only for those who will yet turn to follow ME before the last remaining moments then, I must pull away MY children who are loyal, faithful, and see the writing on the wall. Yes, the tiny few who are not put off by pursuing ME against the lusts for the world. This is a mere handful against the vast sea of humanity.

I am True to MY Words and MY Words are now coming to pass as I said they would. I am allowing you a chance to seek ME—surrender to ME. Deny your association with MY enemy and come to MY Side. I will not leave anyone who wants to come along side ME. You are running out of time.

I am ready to bring MY Resplendent Glory to the earth to enrapture MY chosen, to bring them up hither and set them on higher ground.

I want you to come before the door that is open closes for ever more.

This is your LORD and SAVIOR.

ALMIGHTY GOD.

Philippians 2:15: That ye may be blameless and harmless, the sons of GOD, without rebuke, in the midst of a crooked and perverse nation, among whom ye shine as lights in the world;

James 1:17: Every good gift and every perfect gift is from above, and cometh down from the FATHER of lights, with WHOM is no variableness, neither shadow of turning.

Joel 2:28: And it shall come to pass afterward, that I will pour out MY SPIRIT upon all flesh; and your sons and your daughters shall prophesy, your old men shall dream dreams, your young men shall see visions:

Romans 14:12: So then every one of us shall give account of himself to GOD.

Matthew 24:37-39: 37 But as the days of Noah were, so shall also the coming of the SON of man be. 38 For as in the days that were before the flood they were eating and drinking, marrying and giving in marriage, until the day that Noah entered into the ark, 39 And knew not until the flood came, and took them all away; so shall also the coming of the SON of man be.

1 Thessalonians 5:4-6: 4 But ye, brethren, are not in darkness, that that day should overtake you as a thief. 5 Ye are all the children of light, and the children of the day: we are not of the night, nor of darkness. 6 Therefore let us not sleep, as do others; but let us watch and be sober.

Revelation 4:1: After this I looked, and, behold, a door was opened in heaven: and the first voice which I heard was as it were of a trumpet talking with me; which said, Come up hither, and I will shew thee things which must be hereafter.

Matthew 25:10: And while they went to buy, the bridegroom came; and they that were ready went in with him to the marriage: and the door was shut.

Sun, 30 Dec 2012

The LORD's Words: "I am calling you out, to be separate from the world and the ways of the world."

The LORD's Words for Today (Posted at www.End-Times-Prophecy.Com)

Dear Faithful Friends of CHRIST:

Who is CHRIST Returning for?

In March 2009, the LORD told me to warn others HE was coming back soon to rapture HIS people. Then (August 2010), out of anguish from frustration that it seemed no one was listening to me, a year later I was alone in my car, I asked the LORD just why no one was paying attention to the message HE told me to give the people? The LORD spoke to me on the spot—HE said: "Very few people have been around for the big moves of GOD: very few were saved from Sodom & Gomorrah; very few were saved during Noah's time; very few believed JESUS was GOD when HE walked the earth; and very few will be raptured." Then I was stunned when I came across this verse the very next day which was essentially the same message: Luke 17:26-30: 26 And as it was in the days of Noah, so shall it be also in the days of the SON of man. 27 They did eat, they drank, they married wives, they were given in marriage, until the day that Noah entered into the ark, and the flood came, and destroyed them all. 28 Likewise also as it was in the days of Lot; they did eat, they drank, they bought, they sold, they planted, they builded; 29 But the same day that Lot went out of Sodom it rained fire and brimstone from heaven, and destroyed them all. 30 Even thus shall it be in the day when the SON of man is revealed.

And since the time this Word came to me from GOD about very few being raptured, the LORD has told me on different occasions that only "a remnant"..."a handful"..."a morsel compared to a banquet"...will be raptured.

Most recently (December 25, 2012), the LORD told me HE is only coming back for those who are sitting on the edge of their seats looking for HIS Return.

How many people do you know who are sitting on the edge of their seats watching for the LORD versus people who are sitting back comfortably in their chairs clinging to this world to the point that they want to argue with you about the message that CHRIST's Return is soon?

New Testament Christians spoke of watching for the LORD—they were earnestly looking for CHRIST's Return as you would a cherished long missing loved one—how much more should we in these end times (we know these are the end times because the world is rejecting CHRIST) be earnestly watching? If you aren't sitting on the edge of your seat looking for CHRIST's Return—you aren't just disinterested in the rapture event—you are altogether disinterested in the heart of CHRIST and you had better examine your heart because the LORD wants a church who is LONGING FOR HIS RETURN.

Surrender your ALL—everything including your own personal future plans putting them into the LORD's Capable Hands and allow the LORD to renew your mind as in this scripture: Romans 12:2: And be not conformed to this world: but be ye transformed by the renewing of your mind, that ye may prove what is that good, and acceptable, and perfect, Will of GOD. Ask the LORD for you to be baptized by the HOLY SPIRIT to receive a FULL OIL LAMP (exchanging your life for the fullness of the HOLY SPIRIT). Then when the Will of GOD takes hold of your life because you have given GOD full control, the LORD will show you that the world is bland compared to HIS Great Love and Plans for your life. The LORD will put a hunger in your heart to watch eagerly for HIS Return and your heart will be on the edge of its seat.

Mark 12:30: And thou shalt love the LORD thy GOD with all thy heart, and with all thy soul, and with all thy mind, and with all thy strength: this is the first commandment.

1 Thessalonians 5:4: But ye, brethren, are not in darkness, that that day should overtake you as a thief.

1 Peter 4:18: And if the righteous scarcely be saved, where shall the ungodly and the sinner appear?

Matthew 22:14: For many are called, but few are chosen.

Matthew 7:14: Because strait is the gate, and narrow is the way, which leadeth unto life, and few there be that find it.

Below the LORD's Letters are new visions and an important message about the Mark of the Beast. At the very bottom of this letter is a list of the past letters from the LORD covering many important topics relevant to the times we are living in. Also below is an invitation to download and read the FREE Marriage Supper of the Lamb Ebook with Words from the LORD for this end time generation. THIS BOOK IS CHANGING LIVES! THE MP3 AUDIO VERSION of the Marriage Supper of the Lamb are now available in this letter plus links to Spanish Version of the book. Plus sign up to receive the hottest ever end times headlines coming across our desks in the End Times News Report we put out each week. Plus the latest words/visions from young brothers Jonathan and Sebastian and Buddy Baker. Also, to read past letters from the LORD you can visit this link: http://end-times-prophecy.com/blog/?category_name=2012-the-lords-messages

10. There Is No Other By Which You Can Be Saved

"Don't leave anything to chance—come to MY Saving Arms."

(Words Received from Our LORD by Susan, December 25, 2012)

Let US begin:

Soon, the world will see the Beauty of Truth - Truth that is unfaltering...Truth that is Ever Lasting - MY Truth is consistent, it does not sway - it is not double-minded. MY Truth is solid. When I give Words, I follow through. I will bring to pass that which I have spoken. It will be as I have said in MY Book. What GOD has put in motion, no man can stop. MY Coming is on time, on schedule - just as MY Promise that darkness would overtake the world.

The world is a witness to the darkness that is overtaking the world because of its refusal to follow its GOD and rejecting MY Truth, MY Word. Rebellion will lead all astray who follow it. Very few want the Light—the True Light of GOD, the safe passage found by MY Blood Trail coming from the Cross where MY Blood was spilled for the salvation of hopeless men.

MY Blood Trail is the ONLY ROAD to freedom in a dark, lost world. Only MY Blood, MY Way, MY Words, and MY Cleansing through FULL SURRENDER to MY Leadership will lead you on the safe narrow passage out to safety—the Way to MY Glorious Kingdom.

You MUST FOLLOW ME—no other—there is no other by which you can be saved. Many will lead you astray, asunder off the Narrow Path onto a broad road full of lies and deception. Many will flee to roads that look right, thinking they are on the right paths. These are following wrong routes, doctrines, gospels, gods, beliefs: all leading to the destruction of the soul by the plans and schemes of MY enemy. He is your master until the day you turn from him, bend your knee to ME, repent of the sin you have done under his direction while following his evil ways.

Only when you are ready to throw off his evil in your life and desire for a Better MASTER over you, will you find the salvation of your soul, and be safe in your CREATOR's Grasp away from the promise of eternal torment: punishment for rejecting MY Perfect Will for your life and following the evil master of your soul. You can throw off this deceiver and evil seducer at any moment. Call out MY Name for salvation - desire freedom through "deep desire" to be made whole and no longer held captive to do the will of your flesh in rebellion to MY Will.

You stand between your salvation and MY Gift of freedom and life everlasting in MY Glorious Kingdom. Lay down your defenses. Place your life in MY Hands. Allow ME to cover you in MY Blood to release you from the offenses you will be held accountable for when you face a JUST GOD. This is all yours. You must seek ME for it. No one else can do it for you.

You have moments to spare before evil reigns over all of the earth after I remove MY beloved to safety - so many will not have a second chance to salvation as sudden destruction follows this event. Don't leave anything to chance - come to MY Saving Arms.

Many are residing in everlasting hell, torment - even now. Do not think you are beyond falling into the same error. Humble yourself.

Make ME your LORD and MASTER. I will release you from eternal flames in hell. MY Words are solid.

I AM the CHRIST.

THE ONLY HOPE.

I AM HE.

Numbers 23:19: GOD is not a man, that HE should lie; neither the son of man, that HE should repent: hath HE said, and shall HE not do it? Or hath HE spoken, and shall HE not make it good?

Matthew 7:13-14: 13 Enter ye in at the strait gate: for wide is the gate, and broad is the way, that leadeth to destruction, and many there be which go in thereat: 14 Because strait is the gate, and narrow is the way, which leadeth unto life, and few there be that find it.

John 14:6: JESUS saith unto him, I am the WAY, the TRUTH, and the LIFE: no man cometh unto the FATHER, but by ME.

Romans 4:7-8: 7Saying, Blessed are they whose iniquities are forgiven, and whose sins are covered. 8Blessed is the man to whom the LORD will not impute sin.

1 Thessalonians 5:3: For when they shall say, Peace and safety; then sudden destruction cometh upon them, as travail upon a woman with child; and they shall not escape.

Philippians 2:8: And being found in fashion as a man, HE Humbled HIMSELF, and became obedient unto death, even the death of the cross.

"I am calling you out, to be separate from the world and the ways of the world."

(Words Received from Our LORD by Susan, December 26-27, 2012)

I am ready to give you new Words:

Children, your GOD is addressing you:

There is a time coming in which few will listen to Truth, MY Truth, MY Ever Lasting Truth. The world seems so inviting, real, true. It is enticing, it is death. You can live in the world and not be corrupted by it. To do this you must surrender your ALL to ME and be sealed by MY SPIRIT. HIS Sealing will protect you from the temptations of the flesh for the world. It is only by MY Power that you can be fully saved. It is this Saving Power by which your souls are cleaned: made spotless and ready for MY Coming.

Listen to MY Words: All is not lost if you focus on ME. Look away to other baser things and you will surely die. The hour remaining before MY Approach is narrow just like the road it takes to find ME. You don't have much time to make your way down a road few find.

This means you must SURRENDER FULLY your life to ME. Time is running out and few are making themselves free from the entanglements of this life leading them astray. Given the little time remaining, and the requirements of a wrinkle-free spotless gown I demand of MY bride, you must drop all your earthly idols and focus squarely on your SAVIOR, CREATOR, GOD.

Your attention is diverted and focused on pathways heading to hell—although they look good to you, these routes are leading you into eternal darkness where there is no hope to recover.

December 27, 2012:

I will give you the remainder of the Letter:

Children of Light—those who call themselves MINE: come to your FATHER, your LORD, bend low, humble yourself, show yourself worthy of MY Blood-Bought Salvation by throwing off the old man. Discard your past, repent of your sin committed by the direction of MY enemy and by the evil desire of your heart. I renew the minds of those who lay low before ME in humble submission with a desire to have ME as LORD and MASTER. These are the children I acknowledge. These are the ones who will come out with ME when I pull MY bride free.

Lose yourself to find ME and MY Perfect Will for your life. Let ME make your vessel clean no matter what the circumstances or the damage done to your soul by MY enemy. I am the HEALER of hearts, minds, and bodies. I cure the broken hearts making them whole. I have the answers. I rule over those who put ME in charge of them and set them free to love, laugh, and live in peace and harmony with GOD, their CREATOR.

Blessed are the humble who love their GOD more than the world, more than mammon. They shall see their GOD. All others will be cast away for eternity to outer darkness: forever lost apart from GOD. Soon, I am coming to retrieve the small number who truly pursue their GOD with all their heart, mind, soul, and strength. These numbers are few. Only a few have turned their lives over to ME fully to use at MY Will for MY Purposes.

Soon the world will know what it means to choose against ME and MY Will, GOD's Perfect Will. The world will see what it means to be separated from a Holy GOD when MY people who represent ME on earth are removed from among them. Then horror will consume the earth as the protection I afford MY own will no longer be given the earth and destruction will befall those left behind.

Come into the Light now out of harm's way. I am calling you out, to be separate from the world and the ways of the world. You will be without excuse if you remain behind to face what is coming.

Surrender your pride. Submit to MY Leadership. Learn the Ways of GOD. You are seconds away from disaster. Don't allow pride to rule in your heart to your destruction and eternal loss. Think this over carefully.

THIS IS THE LORD.

GREAT IN HUMILITY.

GREAT IN SALVATION.

Matthew 7:21-23: 21Not every one that saith unto me, LORD, LORD, shall enter into the kingdom of heaven; but he that doeth the will of MY FATHER which is in heaven. 22Many will say to me in that day, LORD, LORD, have we not prophesied in THY Name? And in THY Name have cast out devils? And in THY Name done many wonderful works? 23And then will I profess unto them, I never knew you: depart from ME, ye that work iniquity.

Matthew 7:14: Because strait is the gate, and narrow is the way, which leadeth unto life, and few there be that find it.

Ephesians 4:30: And grieve not the HOLY SPIRIT of GOD, whereby ye are sealed unto the day of redemption.

Ephesians 5:27: That HE might present it to HIMSELF a glorious church, not having spot, or wrinkle, or any such thing; but that it should be holy and without blemish.

Matthew 5:8: Blessed are the pure in heart: for they shall see GOD.

You Will Never Find A Greater Love Than Mine

Thu, 3 Jan 2013

The LORD's Words: A LOVE LETTER

The LORD's Words for Today (Posted at www.End-Times-Prophecy.Com)

Words of the LORD:

"I am the Ever Flowing SOURCE of all that men truly long for in their depraved, empty hearts."

(Words Received from Our LORD by Susan, December 30, 2012)

WE May Begin:

I am YAHUSHUA, your LORD and SAVIOR. I died an agonizing death for all humanity: to fulfill MY Promise to all mankind; to bring down MY enemy; to set the captives free; to show MYSELF Great in all the universe; to show MY Kindness, MY Love, MY Unfailing Radical Love. I gave all—no small task. I bled, MY Blood was shed and it was given in humble submission by a Great KING of all the universe.

I left MY Home on high, lowered MYSELF in a great act of humility taking the form of a human to show forth MY Great Love to MY creation, to demonstrate the Heart of GOD toward those who would receive ME throughout eternity for all those past and to come who need a SAVIOR. This was the height of MY Love—a Love that cannot be contained, held back, or pent up.

MY Love is a flood, a deluge, a powerful force. Once you come near ME and experience MY Love after you surrender your all to ME you will be changed by the Love that flows freely to you. It is unending. It never stops, it does not come short. It is solid, ferocious, a sweeping wave: love that cannot be found anywhere else though men try. The world will come up short though passions flare for a time in worldly pursuits, the coals die off because this world does not offer True LOVE, Love that is resilient, uncompromising, unfaltering, undying, eternal flame. That is MY Love. I am LOVE—all other loves only copy that which is MINE to give; created from the Heart of GOD copied by a fallen world, but always falling short because the source doesn't come from love's CREATOR: the True SOURCE of LOVE Everlasting.

I am HE, I am LOVE. MY Word is LOVE; MY Sacrifice is LOVE Everlasting, a demonstration of the Greatest Show of LOVE. Come live in Love. Be surrounded by the beauty of MY Love—learn MY Ways of Love and Loving: Loving others, forgiving, and living in peace with your GOD.

I have Love you don't know about. It is the Love that is eternal in MY Coming Kingdom of Love. Don't deny yourself Love Everlasting, Pleasures at MY Right Hand, Holiness, Purity, Treasures Laid up, Eternal Love and Companionship with your GOD. Come experience wholeness, beauty, forgiveness, peace. I am the Ever Flowing SOURCE of all that men truly long for in their depraved, empty hearts—always longing, but never satisfied, because they do not seek ME, their GOD, SOURCE of Love, SOURCE of All Truth.

Come melt in MY Arms—I can be trusted. I am safe. I do not harm. I heal the broken hearted. I seal the wounds of deep past sadness. I am FATHER to the fatherless. HUSBAND to the widows, HEALER to the bleeding, SHEPHERD to the lost, COMFORTER to the weary. I am SIGHT to the blind, I am STRENGTH to the weak, I am FRIEND to the lonely, I am SALVATION to the sinner.

You will never find a greater love than MINE. It does not exist though men look and seek for it. I am LOVE. Where else can you find True Love? Many have separated themselves from this Great LOVE. The road is narrow to the Great Broad Endless LOVE. Those who discover this Narrow Path will never die.

This is YAHUSHUA...LOVE ETERNAL

Luke 4:18: The SPIRIT of the LORD is upon ME, because HE hath anointed ME to preach the gospel to the poor; HE hath sent ME to heal the brokenhearted, to preach deliverance to the captives, and recovering of sight to the blind, to set at liberty them that are bruised,

John 10:17: Therefore doth MY FATHER love ME, because I lay down MY Life, that I might take it again.

Psalm 16:11: THOU wilt shew me the path of life: in THY Presence is fulness of joy; at THY Right Hand there are pleasures for evermore.

Matthew 7:14: Because strait is the gate, and narrow is the way, which leadeth unto life, and few there be that find it.

Fri, 11 Jan 2013

The LORD's Words: The churches are the devil's playground

The LORD's Words for Today (Posted at www.End-Times-Prophecy.Com)

Dear Faithful Followers of CHRIST:

We know we are in the end times because the world is turning its back to GOD and we can see horrendous evil going on and that same evil that causes us to be incensed is the same exact evil force inside us that causes us to lie or hurt others. We so easily hurt our family, friends, and co-workers in little ways and we do not even give it a second thought. Then we watch the news and see somebody taking a hostage or killing their own family and themselves and we shudder in horror thinking we cannot relate to this kind of incredible evil. Yet GOD's rule of order says all of our righteousness is as filthy rags apart from HIM.

To GOD a little sin is not okay any more than a lot of sin is wrong. If GOD did not call all sin wrong—no matter how small in our eyes—then where precisely does HE draw the line? How much sin is okay and how much sin is overboard? That is how humans judge. Each person creates in his or her mind their own ratio factoring of what amount of sin is acceptable and what is not.

One man may cheat on his wife without concerns and then watch the nightly news and think that what he sees is shockingly wrong. That is what Hollywood does all the time. The heroes fighting so-called evil foes are cursing and sleeping with women they just met and we look on as if this is normal and acceptable. However to GOD, all sin is evil including swearing and adultery. Yes, terrorism is blatantly evil, but so is the way I hurt someone's feelings when I am inconsiderate. The same evil force is at play in both situations and to GOD sin is sin.

GOD's mercy (receiving forgiveness we do not deserve) and grace (receiving a gift we do not deserve) is also outrageous. We need GOD's forgiveness and grace through the Blood of CHRIST whether we hurt someone's feelings or whether we commit an act of violence. Amazingly, because all sin is offensive to GOD, the precious and ever-available Blood of CHRIST can equally forgive a white lie as well as someone else's shocking heinous crime. Thank GOD for the precious Blood of CHRIST.

When we surrender our lives to CHRIST and invite the HOLY SPIRIT to come fully into our lives, the HOLY SPIRIT will come in and help us to fight the satanic evil that terrorizes and incites everyone to commit evil acts: both big and small. Men cannot discern all the evil in their lives apart from GOD and they cannot see that even small things are outrageous and wrong to our Just and Holy Pure GOD. I am thankful that GOD is the Ultimate JUDGE and not men in their distorted and confused human value systems. I thank GOD that we can turn to HIM for Truth and direction for our lives and we have but to ask HIM for it.

GOD is the Perfect JUDGE because HE sees all, knows all, and even knows the inner hearts and motives of men so then HE is able to render absolute, undeniable true justice.

The evangelist Charles H. Spurgeon wrote in his book "According to Promise" this statement about GOD and sin:

Neither doth the LORD deal with men according to the measure of their moral ability. "Oh," says the seeker, "I think I might be saved if I could make myself better, or become more religious, or exercise greater faith; but I am without strength, I cannot believe; I cannot repent; I cannot do anything right!" Remember, then, that the Gracious GOD has not promised to bless you according to the measure of your ability to serve HIM, but according to the riches of HIS grace as declared in HIS Word. If HIS gifts were bestowed according to your spiritual strength, you would get nothing; for you can do nothing without the LORD.

Very Few Will Be Rescued Out To My Kingdom.

Words of the LORD:

"Even your good works are like filthy rags if you are outside of MY Perfect Will."

(Words Received from Our LORD by Susan, January 4, 2013)

Yes Susan, I would like to give MY people Words:

Children, it is I, your LORD: There is a new day coming. It is coming right around the bend - it is a day that holds great pleasure for many and for many more it holds disaster, darkness, evil.

I cannot lie to you: very few will be rescued out to MY Kingdom. Very few will be found worthy. Very few want MY Ways. Very few want to surrender completely to their GOD. There is only a very small number who actually want to follow MY Ways: to lead the life I require of them.

This is what I require: I want a life that is surrendered to ME FULLY. I want people who lay their life down before ME, who are willing to give ME everything: those who no longer desire the control of MY enemy and running apart from GOD.

MY children who follow their GOD must decide to turn their backs to all their plans for the distant future and to lay all they have at MY Feet. I want a COMPLETE and FULL SURRENDER. These children must decide for themselves that they desire MY Will, MY Leading, MY Control over their lives - their every move.

Very few want to walk this narrow path. Only a few believe their GOD knows best about their life and their comings and goings. I must be made MASTER and LORD FULLY so that you are in MY Perfect Will and can live out the life plan I have staked out for you that leads you on the narrow path to MY Kingdom, MY Eternal Kingdom for those who love their GOD above all else. Only these on the path of righteousness and in the Perfect Will of GOD will be saved.

Children, you can come into MY Will: follow MY Precepts; walk with your GOD; seek MY Face; learn of humility; bear fruit for your GOD OR you can continue to follow the ways of evil against a HOLY GOD. If you are not FULLY SURRENDERED you are working against ME. You are bringing down MY Kingdom on earth and you are affecting the lives of those around you. Even your good works are like filthy rags if you are outside of MY Perfect Will.

If you continue to reject ME, to pursue your own ways and will, I will leave you behind or worse, you may find yourself in sudden destruction apart from GOD then for eternity. Those left behind after I retrieve MY church will face tyranny and the madness of MY enemy. Absolutely no one left behind will "not suffer." All will know the suffering of great tribulation that will leave no one untouched—it will be considered great and complete in its hand of destruction, terror, and torment.

Come now to salvation, rescue assuredness, wholeness of heart and spirit to dwell with your Ever Lasting GOD. SURRENDER your ALL. Give ME everything - ALL or nothing. This is what I require. Read MY Word - test these Words. I am a GOD of Truth.

I AM COMING. BE READY.

This is your LORD and MAKER,

GOD ALMIGHTY.

Matthew 7:13: Enter ye in at the strait gate: for wide is the gate, and broad is the way, that leadeth to destruction, and many there be which go in thereat:

Matthew 24:37: But as the days of Noah were, so shall also the coming of the SON of man be.

Isaiah 64:6-7: But we are all as an unclean thing, and all our righteousnesses are as filthy rags; and we all do fade as a leaf; and our iniquities, like the wind, have taken us away. 7 And there is none that calleth upon THY Name,that stirreth up himself to take hold of THEE: for THOU hast hid THY Face from us, and hast consumed us, because of our iniquities.

1 Thessalonians 5:3: For when they shall say, Peace and safety; then sudden destruction cometh upon them, as travail upon a woman with child; and they shall not escape.

Matthew 24:21: For then shall be great tribulation, such as was not since the beginning of the world to this time, no, nor ever shall be.

11. The Churches Are The Devil's Playground

"The churches are the devil's playground."

(Words Received from Our LORD by Susan, January 8, 2013)

Yes daughter, I will give you new Words:

Children of the MOST HIGH GOD:

MY Approach is nearing. Many believe I am a liar. They believe this in their hearts. MY Book outlines MY Truth which is even now coming to pass. The hour of MY Return is coming and the people want to reject MY Truth. They are blind guides leading the blind. Worse than rejecting the Truth themselves, they are leading others astray also: MY own people who call themselves by MY Name.

They sit comfortably in their homes denying MY Words, while the world around them is going to hell and they along with them, instead of coming into MY Will and allowing ME to use their lives to save others. The penalty will be swift and great for the lukewarm church who passes off religion in exchange for the Truth by the leading of MY HOLY SPIRIT.

The devil works in the church. The churches are the devil's playground. He moves stealthily through the churches cloaked as an angel of light: deceiving, misleading, abusing, tearing down, and dragging people to hell by false words and confusion. Many, many will fall by the wayside within the walls of today's churches at the hands of wolves in sheep's clothing.

Why is it so? Because the lukewarm church refuses to believe I am a GOD WHO requires repentance, fear of GOD, discipline, full surrender, shunning the pursuit of the world and its ways. If you find these Words harsh—they are Loving. I am a Loving GOD. I am also JUST, RIGHTEOUS, and TRUE. I stand for Truth and MY Judgment will be True when you stand before ME. Even if you have followed wrong and misleading counsel, I will still judge correctly because all are accountable for themselves. Each person is responsible for his own salvation: for seeking Truth, for pursuing GOD.

All the answers are available for those who want them. They reside in MY Words, in MY Book and through seeking the counsel of MY HOLY SPIRIT by spending time with ME in the secret place. I am not hard to find, but choices must be made and only you can make them. You must desire ME and MY Truth more than the lies of the world—you cannot serve two masters.

Time is running out. Darkness closes in. Choose WHO you will serve. Satan is a cruel master. His road leads to hell and eternal destruction and torment. I cannot lie, this is where you will go apart from a FULL SURRENDER to ME, your LORD and SAVIOR. Find ME and find your way.

TRUTH Has Spoken.

Romans 14:12: So then every one of us shall give account of himself to GOD.

Galatians 1:14-16: 14 And profited in the Jews' religion above many my equals in mine own nation, being more exceedingly zealous of the traditions of my fathers. 15 But when it pleased GOD, WHO separated me from my mother's womb, and called me by HIS grace, 16 To reveal his SON in me, that I might preach HIM among the heathen; immediately I conferred not with flesh and blood:

1 Corinthians 2:12-14: 12 Now we have received, not the spirit of the world, but the SPIRIT which is of GOD; that we might know the things that are freely given to us of GOD. 13Which things also we speak, not in the words which man's wisdom teacheth, but which the HOLY GHOST teacheth; comparing SPIRITUAL things with SPIRITUAL. 14 But the natural man receiveth not the things of the

SPIRIT of GOD: for they are foolishness unto him: neither can he know them, because they are SPIRITUALLY discerned.

Matthew 6:24: No man can serve two masters: for either he will hate the one, and love the other; or else he will hold to the one, and despise the other. Ye cannot serve GOD and mammon.

Psalm 91:1: He that dwelleth in the secret place of the MOST HIGH shall abide under the Shadow of the ALMIGHTY.

Sat, 19 Jan 2013

The LORD's Words: "Only those who are FULLY committed to ME will feel safe now."

The LORD's Words for Today (Posted at www.End-Times-Prophecy.Com)

Dear Faithful Followers of CHRIST:

The world is becoming increasingly darker: the politics; the things people call "entertainment"; the way people are indifferent and cold-hearted toward others; the rejection of GOD and moral leadership in all nations; the worldwide economic downward spiral; the embracing of humanistic/atheistic/paganistic/satanistic cultural views; the world's overall obvious leaning toward antichrist thinking and the rejection of the Will of GOD—to name a few…

Almost daily I receive letters from people who are troubled by a dark future outlook as well as a myriad of challenges people are facing in their personal lives. Most specifically—the bride of CHRIST and those truly seeking GOD are getting beat up by the enemy. LISTEN to me: you are not alone in your struggles. Don't think it strange that your life seems in a turmoil…LOT'S OF GOD'S PEOPLE ARE GETTING RAKED OVER THE COALS. The enemy is in his LAST hour and he wants to torment GOD's people and those who are turning away from darkness back to light.

I am writing about this because I don't want people to think they are running solo in this incredible war the enemy is waging on those who are truly seeking GOD in these closing moments before the LORD returns and darkness completely envelopes the earth. HANG IN THERE—Cover yourself in the BLOOD of CHRIST—the BLOOD IS INVINCIBLE.

Not quite a year ago, the LORD led me to do a 40-day water fast in a secluded location. I thought it was only about dealing with personal issues at first (yes, the LORD did deal with my personal stuff)—however, I did not know that HE was planning to dictate to me a series of letters that would later become a powerful book that would warn many people about HIS soon coming and end times preparation. (The book is called the MARRIAGE SUPPER OF THE LAMB and you can get it free, downloaded here: https://www.smashwords.com/books/view/162979)

As I began to go through this fasting, I knew that the letters I received daily were very important to the LORD and I knew that I just had to make it through for the full 40 days. Into week four, with still another week to go was such a huge struggle. I looked in the mirror wondering if there would be anything left of me at the end and how this would upset my family and my son in particular. But I knew that GOD was with me and that I was probably in the safest place I could be—right where the LORD had called me to be. My family and friends really were concerned, but I just knew GOD would get me through it. The reason I am bringing this up is at my lowest point when I thought I could not make it through this thing—I thought to myself: "There must be a million people in hell who would trade places with me in this 40-day fast." That thought spurred me on. And now I am telling you—that no matter how rough your current situation is (not to make light of it) there are millions in hell who would trade places with you now. So, have courage—the LORD is with you if you are with HIM. Don't give up—don't stop praying for those around you. NEVER GIVE UP. (The LORD gave me this scripture for you now: Psalm 23:4: Yea, though I walk through the valley of the shadow of death, I will fear no evil: for thou art with me; thy rod and thy staff they comfort me.)

Few Know My Word And Practice My Ways

Words of the LORD:

"It is an abomination to believe the plans of men over your GOD."

(Words Received from Our LORD by Susan, January 12, 2013)

I am ready to bring you Words:

Children, MY coming is nigh. I am warning but few are listening. They would rather listen to men speak about the future—this is evil apart from GOD—apart from MY Words, Truth. I have laid out MY Plans and the signs to watch for: instead you choose to watch what men believe the future holds. This is evil. It is an abomination to believe the plans of men over your GOD.

MY Word says to watch when you see all the signs I have given come to pass, yet you choose to believe lowly men who never pursue their GOD: WHO Knows what the future of men hold. Do they consult ME? Seek MY Face? Practice MY Ways? Read MY Word? Or do they listen to each other's evil schemes, even seeking the words of the dead and demonic. This is a tyranny to MY Kingdom. Evil is running high and wide across the land.

Few know MY Word and practice MY Ways. Few want Truth and prescribe to the Word of GOD. All that men need is laid out in MY Word. It is complete in its instruction for lost and floundering men. Anyone who wants to find ME can find ME in MY Word, but each must have a desire to press in and lay down the distractions of the world in exchange for the knowledge available in MY Teachings: through MY Word and the HOLY SPIRIT, WHO leads you in understanding MY Word. There is no other way. It is not through the understanding of men who they, themselves are apart from GOD. This is not how you will understand MY Word. All knowledge of MY Word can be pursued by those who have hungry hearts and surrender their lives, making ME FULL LORD and MASTER.

I am the ONE WHO Leads and Directs the way along the narrow path. Don't be deceived. All other teachings of men apart from MY SPIRIT will lead you astray down dark broad paths of destruction, eternal hell. Come into MY Light. Seek the Eternal Lamp and Oil of MY HOLY SPIRIT so that you will not lack saving knowledge.

MY coming is soon. MY coming is sure. Don't be found when I come without a full oil lamp. These are dark days. You need your lamp oil full. Many will scramble to know ME after I take out MY church. It will be a dark time for the church left behind. Choose now to avoid what is coming. If you disregard MY Warnings you will face the consequences of your decision. I must tell the Truth.

This is the LORD WHO Knows the Future...

James 4:13-14: 13 Go to now, ye that say, Today or tomorrow we will go into such a city, and continue there a year, and buy and sell, and get gain: 14 Whereas ye know not what shall be on the morrow. For what is your life? It is even a vapour, that appeareth for a little time, and then vanisheth away.

Isaiah 31:1: Woe to them that go down to Egypt for help; and stay on horses, and trust in chariots, because they are many; and in horsemen, because they are very strong; but they look not unto the HOLY ONE of Israel, neither seek the LORD!

Deuteronomy 18:10-12: 10 There shall not be found among you any one that maketh his son or his daughter to pass through the fire, or that useth divination, or an observer of times, or an enchanter, or a witch. 11 Or a charmer, or a consulter with familiar spirits, or a wizard, or a necromancer. 12 For all that do these things are an abomination unto the LORD: and because of these abominations the LORD thy GOD doth drive them out from before thee.

1 Corinthians 2:13-14: 13 Which things also we speak, not in the words which man's wisdom teacheth, but which the HOLY GHOST teacheth; comparing SPIRITUAL things with SPIRITUAL. 14 But the natural man receiveth not the things of the SPIRIT of GOD: for they are foolishness unto him: neither can he know them, because they are SPIRITUALLY discerned.

Hosea 4:6: MY people are destroyed for lack of knowledge: because thou hast rejected knowledge, I will also reject thee, that thou shalt be no priest to ME: seeing thou hast forgotten the law of thy GOD, I will also forget thy children.

Matthew 25:4: But the wise took oil in their vessels with their lamps.

12. Evil Is Even Invading The Places That Should Be Safe

"Only those who are FULLY committed to ME will feel safe now."

(Words Received from Our LORD by Susan, January 14, 2013)

I will give you words for the people:

These are trying times for my people. The evil is enclosing them. There is evil at every turn. Even the safe places are getting dark.

Evil is even invading the places that should be safe. MY people, MY church, those I call MY bride: I want you to know I am with you. I know you feel like you are alone and there are very few that understand you. Do not fear. I am always with you no matter where you go. This is not the hour to be filled with fear.

You are MY people, MY true bride. I will not let the enemy come between us, if you give ME your ALL. Surrender your ALL and live in peace. This is where you can find peace, even in the storm.

The storm clouds are rolling in. Evil is now at every corner. Only those who are FULLY committed to ME will feel safe now: only those who keep their eye and focus on ME. Everyone else will live with the uneasiness of a world that is growing very dark with a future that looks very dark.

There is trouble brewing, make no mistake. Darkness is closing in. But these dark clouds do not have to be over you. I can release you from this overwhelming fear of the future, if you surrender your ALL to ME and trust ME with ALL your ways.

I am the Great EMANCIPATOR. I can free you from the plans of the enemy who wants to lead you and everyone around you into darkness, destruction, and death. I am a GOD ready to liberate, ready to protect, ready to bring you into safety, but you must desire this from ME. I cannot force you into this shelter, although MY Arms are safe and I am the SAFE ROUTE, the NARROW PATH. You must decide to follow ME.

Don't be dismayed. I do offer the light at the end of the tunnel. Follow ME to safety, a peace everlasting, a haven of rest, and safe keeping even in the darkest hour. I am a STRONG TOWER in dark times. Turn to ME before it is too late. Let me rescue you, be among MY church, MY bride. These Words are for your comfort in these difficult days.

This is your LORD, SAVIOR, and RESCUER.

Proverbs 18:10: The Name of the LORD is a STRONG TOWER: the righteous runneth into it, and is safe.

1 John 4:18: There is no fear in love; but perfect love casteth out fear: because fear hath torment. He that feareth is not made perfect in love.

Luke 21:26: Men's hearts failing them for fear, and for looking after those things which are coming on the earth: for the powers of heaven shall be shaken.

Date: Mon, 28 Jan 2013

The LORD's Words: "This is MY lukewarm church—the adulterous flavor in MY Mouth will cause ME to spit her out."

On Monday, January 28, 2013 at 12:53 AM, "In Love with the Whirlwind" <kidsmktg@sbcglobal.net> wrote:

The LORD's Words for Today (Posted at www.End-Times-Prophecy.Com)

Dear Faithful Followers of CHRIST:

When we look out beyond ourselves we can look to the LORD and find LIGHT. But imagine, GOD WHO is perfect, pure, righteous—when HE looks out beyond HIMSELF what does HE see if HE is the only source of LIGHT? This is why I believe it is so important to GOD for HIS creation to empty itself of "self" to make room for HIS LIGHT—the filling of the HOLY SPIRIT in the person who surrenders completely to make CHRIST LORD and MASTER. GOD looks out beyond HIMSELF and then sees a reflection of HIMSELF in HIS OWN creation and this must be very pleasing to HIM.

Have you surrendered your ALL to the LORD allowing HIM to fill you with HIS SPIRIT completely? You just have to repent of your sins and ask the LORD from a heart that truly desires to be in the perfect Will of GOD.

The BELOVED.

(Scripture from King James Version)

Song of Solomon 5:10: My BELOVED is white and ruddy, the CHIEFEST AMONG TEN THOUSAND.

Luke 23:38: And a superscription also was written over HIM in letters of Greek, and Latin, and Hebrew, This Is The KING of the Jews.

Song of Solomon 5:11: HIS Head is as the most fine gold, HIS Locks are bushy, and black as a raven.

John 19:2: And the soldiers platted a crown of thorns, and put it on HIS Head, and they put on HIM a purple robe,

Song of Solomon 5:12: HIS Eyes are as the eyes of doves by the rivers of waters, washed with milk, and fitly set.

John 17:1: These words spake JESUS, and lifted up HIS Eyes to heaven, and said, FATHER, the hour is come; glorify THY SON, that THY SON also may glorify THEE:

Song of Solomon 5:13: HIS Cheeks are as a bed of spices, as sweet flowers:

Isaiah 50:6: I gave MY Back to the smiters, and MY Cheeks to them that plucked off the hair: I hid not MY Face from shame and spitting.

Song of Solomon 5:13: HIS Lips like lilies, dropping sweet smelling myrrh.

Isaiah 53:7: HE was oppressed, and HE was afflicted, yet HE opened not HIS Mouth: HE is brought as a lamb to the slaughter, and as a sheep before her shearers is dumb, so HE openeth not HIS Mouth.

Song of Solomon 5:14: HIS Hands are as gold rings set with the beryl:

John 20:27: Then saith HE to Thomas, Reach hither thy finger, and behold MY Hands;

Song of Solomon 5:14: HIS Belly is as bright ivory overlaid with sapphires.

John 20:27: and reach hither thy hand, and thrust it into MY Side: and be not faithless, but believing.

Song of Solomon 5:15: HIS Legs are as pillars of marble, set upon sockets of fine gold:

John 19:33: But when they came to JESUS, and saw that HE was dead already, they brake not HIS Legs:

Song of Solomon 5:15: HIS Countenance is as Lebanon, excellent as the cedars.

Isaiah 52:14: As many were astonished at THEE; HIS Visage was so marred more than any man, and HIS Form more than the sons of men:

Song of Solomon 5:16: HIS Mouth is most sweet: yea, HE is altogether lovely. This is MY BELOVED, and this is MY FRIEND, O daughters of Jerusalem.

Isaiah 53:9: And HE made HIS grave with the wicked, and with the rich in HIS Death; because HE had done no violence, neither was any deceit in HIS Mouth.

Come Wash Your Garments In My Blood

Words of the LORD:

"This is MY lukewarm church—the adulterous flavor in MY Mouth will cause ME to spit her out."

(Words Received from Our LORD by Susan, January 21, 2013)

Daughter let ME give the people new Words:

Children of the MOST HIGH:

The world is growing dim—the LIGHT is diminishing. All that is good and pure and holy is falling to the wayside. MY enemy is destroying all that is good and pure—and replacing it with evil and darkness. He is desensitizing the world to MY Righteousness and what is of most value: the HOLINESS of GOD.

The world is plummeting into deep darkness, outer darkness with its plans and thoughts apart from the ONE TRUE GOD. Soon the world will be dumbstruck when I remove MY church and all that remains is the horror of a world deplete of True Holiness and the Righteousness of GOD.

This nightmare is coming for those who refuse to come into MY Will and will be left behind. Their decision to reject ME now, MY Word, MY Leadership in their life, and their FULL surrender to ME will leave them facing the leadership, tyranny of the unholy alliance of satan, the antichrist, and their false prophet. This alliance will take in the world by demonic deception, leading the world down a blind alley of destruction to eternal hell—the location of the destination of MY enemy. He plans to take so many with him as he can pursue, control, and deceive. He will succeed—many will see destruction and fall into everlasting hell and torment.

The only way to stop him and his blood thirsty rampage will be MY Second Coming when I arrive to earth with MY holy army, MY church, to stop the mouth of the enemy with the Sword of MY Mouth; to chain up and cast him into hell until he is released one thousand years later. His ultimate end will be the Lake of Fire along with the vast majority of humanity that is taken over by the enemy's deception. This, because the people refuse to surrender their personal will to ME, follow the Teachings of MY HOLY SPIRIT by receiving HIS Baptism. Without the Baptism of MY HOLY SPIRIT which comes when MY children willingly surrender their all to ME, they are not ready when I come in Glory to receive MY church.

Asking for salvation is not the same thing. Many have received salvation but have not yet made ME their LORD and MASTER. This is MY lukewarm church—their relationship with ME is tepid and incomplete. I am not their "ALL IN ALL." They handle the Holy only partially along with the world and their partial relationship is like that of a whore who wants their LORD and MASTER a little but wants to go whoring with the world. I am not good enough to submit to in FULL relationship.

This is MY lukewarm church—the adulterous flavor in MY Mouth will cause ME to spit her out. I cannot take her out with ME to MY Holy Kingdom as she will not be a pure bride. Her hands are dirty handling the world every chance she gets with her eyes, her thoughts, her heart. I can't take it. I gave her ALL of ME and she wants to bring the world into our bed. She repulses ME. I am coming soon and I will leave her standing at the altar of her lukewarm churches wondering why her BRIDEGROOM left her behind. She will pine and be forlorn for ME then when she realizes what she has done and that she is left with a cruel lover who will demand her life.

This is what the lukewarm church will face. Come back to ME O' great church of the lukewarm followers. Come wash your garments in MY Blood. Lay your life down. Leave the world behind. Reject MY enemy and the hold he has over you. You are soon going to be left behind. MY coming is swift. Don't be foolish. Fill your oil lamps. Come get priceless oil from your LORD.

I drank of the cup and now I offer you pure oil from the same cup for your lamp. Let ME fill your cup so it runneth over.

This is your BRIDEGROOM.

PURE—HOLY—RIGHTEOUS.

Philippians 2:15: That ye may be blameless and harmless, the sons of GOD, without rebuke, in the midst of a crooked and perverse nation, among whom ye shine as lights in the world;

Revelation 20:1-3: And I saw an angel come down from heaven, having the key of the bottomless pit and a great chain in his hand. 2 And he laid hold on the dragon, that old serpent, which is the devil, and satan, and bound him a thousand years, 3 And cast him into the bottomless pit, and shut him up, and set a seal upon him, that he should deceive the nations no more, till the thousand years should be fulfilled: and after that he must be loosed a little season.

Revelation 20:10: And the devil that deceived them was cast into the lake of fire and brimstone, where the beast and the false prophet are, and shall be tormented day and night forever and ever.

Revelation 2:16: Repent; or else I will come unto thee quickly, and will fight against them with the sword of MY Mouth.

Revelation 3:15-17: 15I know thy works, that thou art neither cold nor hot: I would thou wert cold or hot. 16So then because thou art lukewarm, and neither cold nor hot, I will spue thee out of MY Mouth. 17Because thou sayest, I am rich, and increased with goods, and have need of nothing; and knowest not that thou art wretched, and miserable, and poor, and blind, and naked:

Acts 19

Face Me, Surrender Your All

Words of the LORD:

"Don't be found outside of MY Will or I will reject and cast you away."

(Words Received from Our LORD by Susan, January 22, 2013)

MY children, your LORD Speaketh:

I am coming. Make no mistake, I have promised and what GOD Says, HE Does. Few believe ME—few truly are moved by these Words and encouragement. I know because I see ALL—I know ALL and I see who pursues ME, follows ME, loves ME above ALL else and all others.

There is no shortage of those who pursue the world, who seek answers through those who deny I exist and reject MY Truth. Soon Truth will be hard to come by. Already it is a diminishing commodity. MY Truth is Priceless Gold—its value cannot be measured as MY Truth leads to MY Kingdom of Eternal Life with ALMIGHTY GOD—CREATOR of the Universe. The value of this Truth cannot be measured or calculated. Few seek it although it is available—readily found. Only those ardent for Truth seek it with all their hearts, souls, minds, and strength—those who surrender their ALL and cling to their GOD. These find Truth—a wellspring of peace, wholeness, and eternal salvation.

MY Priceless Truth cannot be replaced or discovered through many paths though many believe it so. There is only ONE TRUE PATH to the ULTIMATE TRUTH: I AM THE WAY—THE NARROW ROAD. FULL surrender to ME: LORD WHO was crucified for the transgressions of all men through acts of sin treason against the Ways of a Holy, Just GOD. I laid MY Life down, gave ALL, endured torture for sin-filled mankind. I was bruised, scourged, spat upon, beaten, and I became the punishment for all men. This was the price MY FATHER would accept for the sins of all men for whosoever would lay their life down, submit themselves over to ME and choose ME as LORD and MASTER.

There is no other way—only MY WAY—MY Gift, MY Price Paid. Although there appears to be many ways, there is only ONE WAY, through ME and the Baptism of the HOLY SPIRIT.

The world is falling apart. All seems well. This is because you refuse to look to see. You must see the hour you live in—time is running out. You must see the times you are living in and to see this you must read MY Book and receive eye salve from MY SPIRIT to receive understanding of the Words you are reading. Only HE can open your eyes to the meaning of the Words in MY Holy Book. This is essential to being ready for what is coming: the rescue of MY ready bride and tribulation meant for those who choose against ME and are left behind.

Face ME, surrender your ALL. Find safe keeping in the Perfect Will of GOD. Don't be found outside of MY Will or I will reject and cast you away.

Come now. Live in peace with your GOD.

I Love you,

LORD YAHUSHUA.

Numbers 23:19:: GOD is not a man, that HE should lie; neither the son of man, that HE should repent: hath HE said, and shall HE not do it? Or hath HE spoken, and shall HE not make it good?

Psalm 85:10: Mercy and truth are met together; righteousness and peace have kissed each other.

1 Corinthians 6:20: For ye are bought with a price: therefore glorify GOD in your body, and in your spirit, which are GOD's.

Matthew 7:21: Not everyone that saith unto ME, LORD, LORD, shall enter into the kingdom of heaven; but he that doeth the Will of MY FATHER which is in heaven.

Prepare for the very soon rapture.

Read all the books by Susan Davis:

Left Behind After The Rapture

Rapture or Tribulation

Marriage Supper of the Lamb

Also by Susan Davis and Sabrina De Muynck

I Am Coming, Volume 1

I Am Coming, Volume 2

I Am Coming, Volume 3

I Am Coming, Volume 4

I Am Coming, Volume 5

I Am Coming, Volume 6

Available as paperbacks and kindle ebooks at:
www.amazon.com

Also available for free as ebooks (various formats) at:
www.smashwords.com

Made in the USA
Monee, IL
29 December 2020